Youth Violence

Editor: Danielle Lobban

Volume 430

First published by Independence Educational Publishers

The Studio, High Green

Great Shelford

Cambridge CB22 5EG

England

© Independence 2023

Copyright

This book is sold subject to the condition that it shall not, by way of trade or otherwise, be lent, resold, hired out or otherwise circulated in any form of binding or cover other than that in which it is published without the publisher's prior consent.

Photocopy licence

The material in this book is protected by copyright. However, the purchaser is free to make multiple copies of particular articles for instructional purposes for immediate use within the purchasing institution. Making copies of the entire book is not permitted.

ISBN-13: 978 1 86168 890 3

Printed in Great Britain

Zenith Print Group

Acknowledgements

The publisher is grateful for permission to reproduce the material in this book. While every care has been taken to trace and acknowledge copyright, the publisher tenders its apology for any accidental infringement or where copyright has proved untraceable. The publisher would be pleased to come to a suitable arrangement in any such case with the rightful owner.

The material reproduced in **issues** books is provided as an educational resource only. The views, opinions and information contained within reprinted material in **issues** books do not necessarily represent those of Independence Educational Publishers and its employees.

Images

Cover image courtesy of iStock. All other images courtesy of Freepik, Pixabay and Unsplash.

Additional acknowledgements

With thanks to the Independence team: Shelley Baldry, Tracy Biram, Klaudia Sommer and Jackie Staines.

Danielle Lobban

Cambridge, September 2023

Contents

Chapter 1: Knife Crime

What is knife crime?	1
Getting a knife is like 'ordering a pizza': the reality of Britain's knife crime epidemic	2
Knife crime statistics	4
Spotlight on: knife crime with the Ben Kinsella trust	6
Pencil cases, water bottles and knives: the back-to-school kit for UK pupils	8
The UK Government wants to crack down on knife crime – research can tell us why young people start carrying weapons	10
#LifeorKnife - the consequences	11
Lives not knives: young people's perspective on knife crime	12

Chapter 2: Gangs & Violence

Gangs and street violence	14
Scouse Soldiers: why do young people get involved in gangs?	16
Up to one in five teenage boys say they or their friends have been offered work by drug gangs, survey finds	18
New figures reveal 12,720 children in England were at risk of criminal exploitation	19
What is county lines?	20
County Lines: what is it and what can we do to tackle it?	21
'How I escaped a County Lines drug gang'	22
Girls in gangs: how they are recruited, exploited and trapped	25

Chapter 3: Tackling Youth Crime

Stop and search	26
When will Sadiq Khan admit that stop and search works?	29
Forgotten voices: policing, stop and search and the perspectives of Black children	30
Boy gangster recruited when he was 12 makes desperate plea for help to get out	31
I was stabbed and surrounded by gangs at school – this is how to stop these attacks	33
Sport can help to reduce youth offending but the evidence around what works is problematic	35
Coalition calls for alternative solutions to serious youth violence	36
What's the solution to youth crime?	38
Agony of mum whose teen son lost his life to knife crime	40

Useful Websites	42
Glossary	43
Index	44

Introduction

Youth Violence is Volume 430 in the **issues** series. The aim of the series is to offer current, diverse information about important issues in our world, from a UK perspective.

About Youth Violence

With an increasing amount of youth violence over the past decade, this book looks at reasons why young people may join gangs and carry weapons. It also explores the effects of youth crime and ways to overcome it.

Our sources

Titles in the **issues** series are designed to function as educational resource books, providing a balanced overview of a specific subject.

The information in our books is comprised of facts, articles and opinions from many different sources, including:

- Newspaper reports and opinion pieces
- Website factsheets
- Magazine and journal articles
- Statistics and surveys
- Government reports
- Literature from special interest groups.

A note on critical evaluation

Because the information reprinted here is from a number of different sources, readers should bear in mind the origin of the text and whether the source is likely to have a particular bias when presenting information (or when conducting their research). It is hoped that, as you read about the many aspects of the issues explored in this book, you will critically evaluate the information presented.

It is important that you decide whether you are being presented with facts or opinions. Does the writer give a biased or unbiased report? If an opinion is being expressed, do you agree with the writer? Is there potential bias to the 'facts' or statistics behind an article?

Activities

Throughout this book, you will find a selection of assignments and activities designed to help you engage with the articles you have been reading and to explore your own opinions. Some tasks will take longer than others and there is a mixture of design, writing and research-based activities that you can complete alone or in a group.

Further research

At the end of each article we have listed its source and a website that you can visit if you would like to conduct your own research. Please remember to critically evaluate any sources that you consult and consider whether the information you are viewing is accurate and unbiased.

Issues Online

The **issues** series of books is complemented by our online resource, issuesonline.co.uk

On the Issues Online website you will find a wealth of information, covering over 70 topics, to support the PSHE and RSE curriculum.

Why Issues Online?

Researching a topic? Issues Online is the best place to start for...

Librarians

Issues Online is an essential tool for librarians: feel confident you are signposting safe, reliable, user-friendly online resources to students and teaching staff alike. We provide multi-user concurrent access, so no waiting around for another student to finish with a resource. Issues Online also provides FREE downloadable posters for your shelf/wall/table displays.

Teachers

Issues Online is an ideal resource for lesson planning, inspiring lively debate in class and setting lessons and homework tasks.

Our accessible, engaging content helps deepen students' knowledge, promotes critical thinking and develops independent learning skills.

Issues Online saves precious preparation time. We wade through the wealth of material on the internet to filter the best quality, most relevant and up-to-date information you need to start exploring a topic.

Our carefully selected, balanced content presents an overview and insight into each topic from a variety of sources and viewpoints.

Students

Issues Online is designed to support your studies in a broad range of topics, particularly social issues relevant to young people today.

Thousands of articles, statistics and infographs instantly available to help you with research and assignments.

With 24/7 access using the powerful Algolia search system, you can find relevant information quickly, easily and safely anytime from your laptop, tablet or smartphone, in class or at home.

Visit issuesonline.co.uk to find out more!

Chapter 1

Knife Crime

What is knife crime?

Knife crime is a serious problem that affects many people, especially young people. Knife crime is any crime that involves a knife or a sharp object. Knife crime can include:

- Carrying a knife or trying to buy one if you are under 18
- Threatening someone with a knife or a sharp object
- Owning a type of knife that is banned by the law
- Injuring or killing someone with a knife or a sharp object
- Intending to harm or injure someone with a knife or a sharp object
- Committing burglary or robbery while carrying a knife as a weapon

A knife is an example of an offensive weapon, which means something that can hurt or harm another person.

Why is knife crime dangerous?

Knife crime is dangerous for many reasons. Firstly, it can cause serious injuries or death to the victims and the attackers. Knife crime can also have long-term effects on the physical and mental health of the people involved and their families and friends.

Secondly, knife crime can create fear and distrust in communities. People may feel unsafe to go out or to socialise with others. Knife crime can also lead to more violence and retaliation, as some people may want to take revenge or to protect themselves.

Thirdly, knife crime can have legal consequences for the offenders. Depending on the type and severity of the offence, they may face prison sentences, fines, community service, or criminal records. Having a criminal record can make it harder to find a job, get an education, or travel abroad in the future.

Why do some people carry knives?

There are different reasons why some people may choose to carry knives. Some of these reasons are:

Peer pressure: Some people may feel pressured by their friends or gangs to carry knives to fit in or to look tough.

Self-defence: Some people may feel scared or threatened by others and think that carrying a knife will make them safer or more confident.

Status: Some people may think that carrying a knife will make them more respected or powerful in their social circles.

Ignorance: Some people may not know the law or the risks of carrying knives.

However, none of these reasons are good enough to justify carrying a knife. Research shows that 99% of young people do not carry knives and that you are more likely to be hurt or injured if you carry one. Carrying a knife does not make you safer or more respected; it makes you more likely to get into trouble or danger.

How can we stop knife crime?

There are many ways that we can help to stop knife crime and make our communities safer. Some of these ways are:

Education: We can learn about the law and the consequences of knife crime from reliable sources, such as teachers, police officers, or websites like Fearless or LiveSafe. We can also learn about how to deal with conflicts peacefully and how to avoid risky situations.

Support: We can seek help from trusted adults, such as parents, teachers, counsellors, or youth workers, if we feel scared, pressured, or tempted to carry knives. We can also support our friends and peers who may be involved in knife crime and encourage them to seek help too.

Reporting: We can report any suspicious or illegal activity involving knives to the police or anonymously through Crimestoppers.

Awareness: We can raise awareness about the dangers and impacts of knife crime in our schools and communities. We can also join campaigns and initiatives that aim to prevent and reduce knife crime, such as No Knives Better Lives in Scotland.

Other organisations who can advise on knife crime, youth violence and gangs are listed on page 42.

Getting a knife is like 'ordering a pizza': the reality of Britain's knife crime epidemic

By Rosie MacLeod

In the summer of 2008, the UK was shocked and saddened by the fatal stabbing of teenager Ben Kinsella in an unprovoked attack. Thirteen years on, his demographic category (young men) remains the most vulnerable to the growing dangers of the blade. There were '285 deaths by a knife or sharp instrument in the 12 months ending March 2018'. Amongst the victims, around 71 (one in four) were male and between the ages of 18-24.

Trust issues, insecurity, and wealth inequality

Ben Kinsella's 16-24 age group is now '45% more likely to suffer knife attacks than in 1946, when records began'.

The rising number of young people that are threatened and traumatised at knifepoint is concerning. Firstly, this could make for a future epidemic of PTSD and mental health problems. Secondly, young people are more naïve, impressionable and likely to fall in with the wrong crowd. Slippery slopes cost futures.

With the above in mind, the social enterprise Inside Success serves to raise awareness of knife violence, especially among the young. One of its volunteers, Israel, explains that 'knife crime and mental health problems are one hundred per cent connected. [...] It's about upbringing. A lot of people have never had a dad in their house. That can also affect mental health'. This helps suggest some underlying reasons for knife possession.

It's argued that toddlers develop trust by forming 'a secure attachment to their parents or caregivers'. This trust becomes 'absolutely necessary' for a child's 'healthy psychological development'.

An absent father cannot show his children what to expect from grown men. Perhaps this leaves them suspicious of their intentions? This may also explain why 'fatherless children have more difficulties with social adjustment, and [...] underlying fears, resentments, anxieties and unhappiness'.

Subsequently, fatherlessness emerges as something with the power to erode trust, leaving a child apprehensive. This echoes Israel's observation that 'people feel exposed, so they carry these knives for protection. And then, when they feel threatened, they try to defend themselves'.

As well as the inability to trust, father absenteeism leaves a person in a single income household. Israel identifies 'inequality of wealth' as one of knife crime's contributing factors. 'If everybody had a stable amount of income, the children would not feel the need to go out and find more. At least not in a way where they'd make a life-altering decision'. Unsurprisingly, robbery is the second most common knife offence after assault.

It is also no coincidence that in 2017, 53 per cent of knife possession suspects were Black: the ethnic group most susceptible to casual or insecure work.

Misleading statistics

The trust set up in Ben Kinsella's name reports 46,937 police-recorded offences with a knife or sharp instrument in the 12 months to June 2021. Just three years earlier in 2018, under 40,000 incidents were recorded – the 'highest level recorded over a year'.

However, at the time of his murder and in the time before, knife crime was much higher than it is now. In 2007/8, 138,000 knife incidents were recorded, making that 6 per cent of all incidents. This is significantly less than the estimated 334,000 in the mid-1990s, accounting for 8 per cent of all incidents.

Statistics show an apparent decrease in knife crime, But to take them at face value would be misleading. While it is true that knife offences are becoming less frequent, the injuries from them are now 'more severe'. Doctors report increasing numbers of women and younger people being affected.

Neither straightforward nor simple

As with many forms of criminality, such as illegal trafficking and misuse of firearms, knife crime is entangled in a heavily underground crime web.

Key Facts

- Males between the ages of 18-24 are the most likely victims of knife crime.
- 16-18-year-olds are 45% more likely to suffer a knife attack than in 1946.
- From June 2020 to June 2021 there were 46,937 police-recorded offences with a knife or sharp instrument.
- In 2007/2008 there were 138,000 police-recorded offences with a knife.

As Israel explains, 'knife crime is mainly an end result, the accumulation of a lot of things. Young people might get involved with drug trafficking before they get stabbed or go and stab someone, and it's something you cannot come back from. You'll owe so many people money.' This brings us to the misleading decreases in knife crime incidents, as shown in official statistics. What they fail to reveal is that they often result from knife victims who 'cannot be seen to be snitching', as explained anonymously by one young man.

There is a vicious circle of more unreported knife incidents and an increased inability of victims to come forward. In this way, crime is driven further and further underground. Its detachment from the wider world is so pronounced that 'it's very easy to get a knife ordered off Amazon to your door. It's like ordering a pizza. There are websites selling zombie knives and samurai swords – not on the dark web'. And this is something that anyone outside the crime circle would simply not think to search for, including the police.

The failure of authorities to document knife offences helps explain their seeming 'decrease'. According to Israel: '[Knife crime] is happening so much now that [police] stations don't really record it. It is more the community addressing the problem, rather than the police. The police aren't doing enough. Most of them didn't really grow up in that sort of environment so they don't know what it's like'.

Different start, different future

What chiefly emerges from speaking to young people in the know about dangerous knife culture are the effects of segregated neighbourhoods. While problems begin at home, they are essentially perpetuated by ignorance owing to different living standards. Young people from the affected areas find it, 'amazing [that] dealing with stab wounds is not common knowledge given how big of a problem it is'. I'm shocked at how casually Israel advises me to 'calm down if you get stabbed – so that you don't lose more blood'. This is normal life for some of us.

The social divide produces feedback loops. Areas with high knife crime will certainly deter visitors from safer areas. Consequently, division and lack of understanding prevail when 'what we need is to unite'. Continued failure to recognise the full extent of Britain's knife crime problem will keep it underground for longer. The longer we wait, the more frightening it becomes.

17 December 2021

The above information is reprinted with kind permission from Shout Out UK.
© 2023 Shout Out UK

www.shoutoutuk.org

Knife crime statistics

An extract from Knife crime in England and Wales: statistics

By Grahame Allen & Matthew Burton

Knife crime is a crime involving an object with a blade or sharp instrument. It is a persistent police priority and disproportionately impacts young people and disadvantaged people.

Offences involving a knife

The Office for National Statistics (ONS) publishes data on crimes recorded by police involving a knife or sharp instrument for a selection of serious violent offences.

In the year ending March 2022, there were around 45,000 offences involving a knife or sharp instrument in England and Wales (excluding Greater Manchester Police Force). This was 9% higher than in 2020/21 and 34% higher

Recent trends in knife crime have been affected by undercounting in the Greater Manchester Police Force area before 2018/19. Increases in recorded offences since 2018/19 are directly related with improvements in recording practices.

Homicide offences

In the year ending March 2022, Home Office data shows there were 261 homicides (currently recorded) using a sharp instrument, including knives and broken bottles. This meant sharp instruments were used in 40% of the 594 homicides that occurred in 2021/22.

Knife crime by police force area

ONS data shows that West Midlands Police Force recorded the highest rate of 152 offences involving a knife per 100,000 population in 2021/22. This is a 3% decrease on a rate of 156 recorded in 2020/21. Dyfed-Powys had the lowest rate of 34 offences per 100,000 individuals (up from 28 in 2020/21).

Proven offences and offenders

Sentencing statistics from the Ministry of Justice shows that in the year ending March 2022, there were 19,555 cautions and convictions made for possession of a knife or offensive weapon. Juveniles (aged 10-17) were the offenders in 18% of cases.

Hospital admissions

Police and courts crime data depends on offences being reported to the authorities, which is a weakness. To get a more rounded view on knife crime it is useful to supplement this information with alternative sources such as NHS hospital data.

Data from NHS Digital shows there were 4,171 'hospital episodes' recorded in English hospitals in 2021/22 due to assault by a sharp object. This was 2% higher than in 2020/21 and 14% higher than in 2014/15.

Offences relating to knife crime

The Library briefing Knives and Offensive Weapons discusses the legislation governing the carrying (possession) and sale of knives and other offensive weapons. The main possession offences are as follows:

It is an offence under Section 1 of the Prevention of Crime Act 1953 for a person to have 'with him in a public place any offensive weapon without lawful authority or reasonable excuse'.

Under Section 139 of the Criminal Justice Act 1988 it is an offence for a person to have 'with him in a public place… any article which has a blade or is sharply pointed', except a folding pocketknife with a cutting edge of three inches or less, without good reason or lawful authority.

Under Section 139A of the Criminal Justice Act 1988, it is an offence for a person to have an offensive weapon or a bladed or pointed article on school premises without good reason or lawful authority.

Selected offences involving a knife or sharp instrument
Year ending March, England and Wales, excluding Greater Manchester (thousands)

Source: Knife crime in England and Wales: statistics

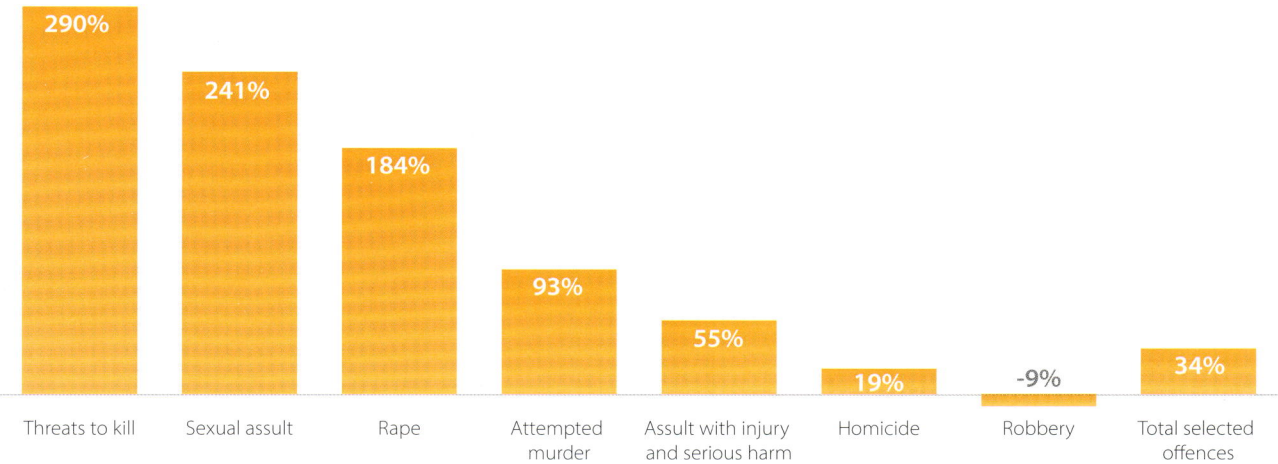

Source: Knife crime in England and Wales: statistics

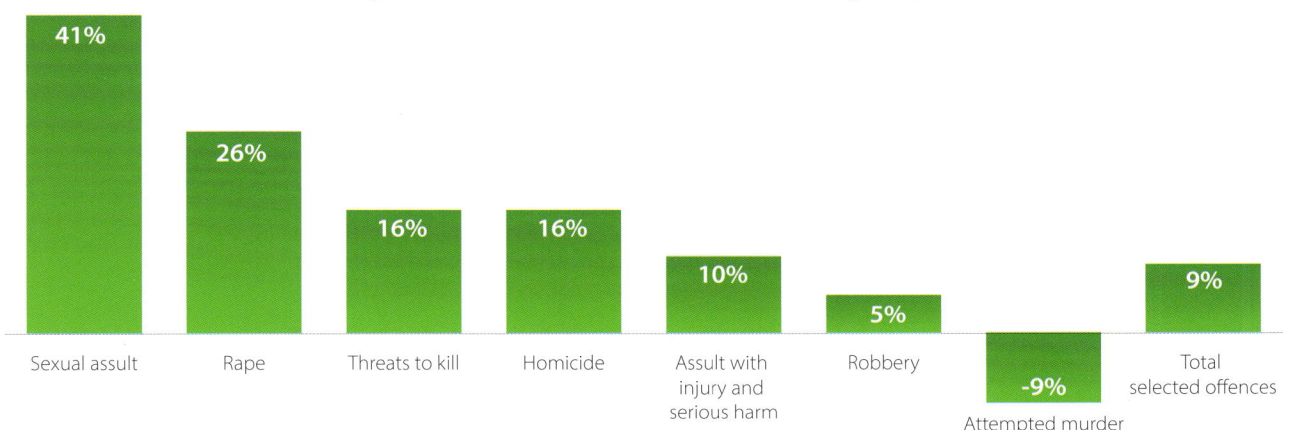

Source: Knife crime in England and Wales: statistics

Trends over time

In 2021/22 there were around 45,400 offences involving a sharp instrument in England and Wales. This was 9.1% higher than in 2020/21 and 33.7% higher than in 2010/11.

The chart on page 4 shows that the number of selected offences involving a knife or sharp object fell between 2010/11 and 2013/14 before rising over the next six years.

The main offences involving a knife or sharp instrument recorded in 2021/22 were assault with injury and intent to cause serious harm (49.9%) and robbery (34.3%). The chart above shows there were more offences committed in all categories (except for robbery) in 2021/22 compared to 2010/11. This data excludes Greater Manchester Police Force.

Since 2010/11, the total number of selected offences involving a knife or sharp instrument has increased by 34% (from around 34,000 to 45,000) and the number of threats to kill using knives or sharp objects has nearly quadrupled (from around 1,400 to 5,500).

During that year, the total number of offences involving a knife or sharp instrument increased by 9% (from 41,600 to 45,400).

Sexual assault involving a knife increased the most (41%, 206 to 290), followed by rape (26%, 542 to 681) and threats to kill and homicide (both 16%, 4,800 to 5,500 and 225 to 261, respectively).

Attempted murder was the only offence category with decrease (of 9%) in the twelve months to March 2022 (460 to 418). Care should be taken when comparing figures for rape, sexual assault, attempted murder and homicide offences over time due to the relatively low number of these offences recorded.

10 January 2023

The above information is reprinted with kind permission from UK Parliament.
© UK Parliament 2023
This information is licensed under the Open Parliament Licence v3.0
To view this licence, visit https://www.parliament.uk/site-information/copyright-parliament/open-parliament-licence/

www.parliament.uk

Spotlight on: knife crime with the Ben Kinsella trust

We're taking a look at is knife crime, and what can be done is stop it. We've partnered with the Ben Kinsella Trust - who educate young people on the dangers of knife crime and help them to make positive choices to stay safe. Here's what they have to say…

TW: violence, death

What is knife crime?

Knife crime is a term commonly used to describe crimes where any shaped or bladed object is used. This includes anything which is intentionally fashioned into a blade for the purpose of inflicting harm.

Let's talk about knife crime.

We can't escape the recurring headlines. It feels as though every day we hear about another senseless killing, another life-changing injury, another family robbed of a beloved member. But despite the seeming prevalence of these stories, most people do not carry a knife. It is not normal to carry a knife.

The statistics around knife crime are stark. In the twelve months to March 2022, 90 people aged under 25 died after being stabbed. That is 90 too many

Who was Ben Kinsella?

Ben Kinsella was just 16 years old when he was killed in an horrific act of senseless knife crime violence on June 29 2008.

Ben had been out at a local pub to celebrate the end of his GCSEs with his friends. On their way home, he and his friends realised they were being followed by three older teenagers. Scared and worried, they decided to run home.

But the older teenagers chased after them. They were seeking revenge for an altercation in the club that had taken place earlier that evening. Ben and his friends had nothing to do with the altercation, but when the older boys caught up with Ben, in an unprovoked attack, they stabbed him to death.

What is the Ben Kinsella Trust?

Ben's family set up the Ben Kinsella Trust in 2008 to educate children and young people about knife crime and to campaign for justice and action for those affected by knife crime.

The Ben Kinsella Trust is now one of the UK's leading anti-knife crime charities. We educate young people on the dangers of knife crime and help them to make positive choices to stay safe. Our workshops and online resources follow the real-life journeys of victims and the offenders through a series of unique and immersive experiences to show how choices and consequences are intrinsically linked.

Knife crime: the myths

There is an incredible amount of misinformation around knife crime. The most common myth is that carrying a knife can protect you from harm. This is simply not true. The fact is that someone carrying a knife is more likely to be killed or injured with their own knife.

Another common myth is that there are safe places on the body to stab someone. Which is simply not true. The human body has a unique and intricate design, with multiple systems, each in place for a specific purpose. Any interruption to any part of this can be fatal. Whilst stabbings often reach the headlines, many thousands of people who survive knife attacks live on, often with life-changing injuries. These stories are not told – the boy who was stabbed in the bowel and has to use a colostomy bag for the rest of his life; the man who had to have his leg amputated after he was stabbed in his femoral artery; the girl who is now registered disabled due to losing the use of her right arm after a stabbing injury; the boy whose brain stem was damaged in a stabbing, meaning he will need twenty-four hour care for the rest of his life. Imagine that these are your friends, your family.

Knife crime does not just affect the victim and the offender. When someone is involved in a knife attack, the impact ripples on for all concerned. In the case of a tragic death after a knife attack, the impact on the family is profound and everlasting; family members never recover. They will forever

Key Facts

- Ben Kinsella, 16, was killed on 29th June 2008.
- In the twelve months to March 2022, 90 people aged under 25 died after being stabbed.
- You can go to prison for up to four years, just for carrying a knife.

reflect on what might have been; they may find themselves blaming themselves, or others; analysing what possible action could have been taken to prevent the senseless loss. Friends grieve the loss forever. Whole communities experience an acute sadness at the injustice of the loss.

Knife crime and the law

Many people do not realise how the law is applied to knife crime cases. In law, someone can go to prison for up to four years, just for having a knife on their person, regardless of the reason. Being convicted for carrying a knife also means that you will have a criminal record. This could affect which countries you can travel to, your employment and education prospects.

But you don't have to carry a knife to be convicted of a crime. If someone is present during a knife attack, and the bystander is judged to have assisted or encouraged the attack in any way, they can be convicted of joint enterprise. Being convicted of joint enterprise means you could serve the same sentence as the offender.

What can I do to stop knife crime?

There are steps that you can take. Knife crime is not normal – most people do not carry a knife. Where people are carrying knives, normalising this behaviour is not okay and we need to challenge it. We all have a responsibility to reach out to our peers to prevent them from being drawn into negative activity. Talk with your friends about the risks around knife crime – one poor decision can result in a life being changed forever; consider the consequences of knife crime and the way in which your life would change. To learn more about how knife crime changed the lives of young people visit the Ben Kinsella Trust Learning Zone. Here you'll find stories from real young people whose lives were changed forever due to knife crime.

We must all take responsibility. Teenagers are losing their lives to knife crime. People are living with stark injuries because of knife attacks. If you have information, share it with a trusted adult, or if that is difficult, share it anonymously with Fearless. You do not want to look back in the future and think 'if only'.

Your life is a unique opportunity to bring about positive change – what are you going to do?

If you have any concerns about knife crime and how it affects you and others around you, or feel like you need to talk to someone about any other issue, you can contact The Mix who offer free information and mental health support to under 25s or contact Childline for free on 0800 1111 or via www.childline.org.uk.

May 2023

Read

Visit the Ben Kinsella Trust Learning Zone and read some real-life stories on the consequences of knife crime.

The above information is reprinted with kind permission from National Citizen Service and The Ben Kinsella Trust.

© 2023 NCS

www.wearencs.com

www.benkinsella.org.uk

Pencil cases, water bottles and knives: the back-to-school kit for UK pupils

By Chante-Marie

We sigh at the senseless gun violence in the US. Many of us marvel at the nation that prioritises protecting their Second Amendment right over the safety of their children. The same children whose trivial fears of being picked last in PE have now been replaced by the prospect of school shootings, and a lifetime of PTSD.

This same frustration, however, does not seem to extend to the countless teenagers who are murdered by their peers in the UK.

Eyes wide shut

Knife crime was initially dismissed as isolated inner-city crime or ethnic hooliganism when this problem became topical in 2018. Now harrowing stories of 12-year-olds fresh from primary school slaughtering each other dominate the news. So will we finally address an epidemic that has reached an all-time boiling point?

In the twelve months between March 2021 and March 2022, 47,167 offences involving a sharp weapon were recorded in England. This marks a 10 per cent increase on the previous year and a 46 per cent increase across England and Wales compared to figures in March 2012.

Despite such worrisome statistics, a study conducted by the National Youth Agency found that: 'whilst more young people are being exposed to and are experiencing crime, less are actively engaged in crime.'

This report is synonymous with the rising reports of young people killed in 'chance encounters' – where the victim is unknown to the perpetrator. Most unforgettably, the murder of 12-year-old Ava White who was fatally stabbed to death last November is one such case.

Chance encounters inflict fear at the core of a community. Unlike gang-related killings, it is impossible to detach from the crime. It feels personal because your child, sister or friend could become the next victim. These random acts of horrific violence entrench mistrust and suspicion within the communities afflicted, inciting hatred for the perpetrators.

Retribution is not the solution

It is easy to criminalise young offenders and resort to calls for punitive measures to gain retribution for those affected. However, as a nation, we need to address the real issue. Children are killing their peers.

When 13- and 14-year-olds can murder, it does not simply reflect a heinous crime but an additional systemic failure to adequately socialise our youth.

Ava White's killer took a life in a senseless and unwarranted attack. However, he also lacked the safety, support and boundaries that a home should provide. Witnessing domestic abuse from a young age, being a victim of assault, and facing exploitation from local crime rings were all factors leading to his ultimate violent act. By the age of fifteen, the boy from a broken home was a convicted murderer.

This is a tale of a boy who succumbed to his environment. To prevent future victims, we must address the positive association between 'adverse childhood experiences and poor mental health' amongst those involved with youth and gang violence.

A study authored by the National Youth Agency (NYA) in 2019 identified three main factors for knife crime:

- Structural issues such as inequality, deprivation and social trust
- Cultural issues such as neighbourhood disorder and exposure to violence
- Loss of year-round and voluntarily accessible youth services.

They also highlighted the influence of prior involvement with crime and the misuse of alcohol and drugs. Unemployment, economic deprivation, exclusion and truancy as well as psychological conditions such as hyperactivity were too seen as key risk factors for knife crime.

Results from the Surveying Prisoner Crime Reduction (SPCR) longitudinal cohort study of prisoners, found that of 1,435 adult prisoners interviewed:

- 24 per cent had been in care at some point during their childhood
- 18 per cent of prisoners stated that they had a family member with an alcohol problem and 14 per cent with a drug problem
- 59 per cent of prisoners stated that they suffered from truancy in school
- 63 per cent had been suspended or temporarily excluded, and 42 per cent stated that they had been permanently excluded or expelled

These statistics strongly indicate that we are failing to protect children who are 'victims of circumstance and in need of safeguarding and positive support.'

A 2019 APPG on Knife Crime Report evidenced a 'correlation between areas where youth services had suffered the largest cuts, and where knife crime had risen the most.'

And the recommendation?

'The Youth Violence Commission also highlights that a well-resourced youth service is necessary in the prevention of knife crime.'

Under austerity, accessible provisions for those who needed state support the most were cut. Between 2008/09 and 2016/17 services to young people faced a 62.25 per cent reduction in spending. Without these services, vulnerable children lack an outlet from the systemic issues that face them.

To prevent further senseless violence, we must introduce early intervention policies to ensure no child is left behind. We should also strive to support rather than merely punish misled young people within the criminal justice system.

Let us learn from the mistakes of the USA. Don't let our children become another statistic.

31 August 2022

The above information is reprinted with kind permission from Shout Out UK.
© 2023 Shout Out UK

www.shoutoutuk.org

Key Facts

- Whilst more young people are being exposed to and are experiencing crime, less are actively engaged in crime.
- 24 per cent of adult prisoners had been in care at some point during their childhood.
- 18 per cent of prisoners stated that they had a family member with an alcohol problem and 14 per cent with a drug problem
- 59 per cent of prisoners stated that they suffered from truancy in school
- 63 per cent of prisoners had been suspended or temporarily excluded from school and 42 per cent stated that they had been permanently excluded or expelled from school.

The UK Government wants to crack down on knife crime – research can tell us why young people start carrying weapons

An article from The Conversation.

By Iain Brennan, Professor of Criminology, University of Hull

The government has lifted restrictions on stop and search powers in an effort to combat knife crime. This approach focuses on people who are already carrying weapons. My research, published late last year, can help explain what happens in young people's lives before they start carrying a weapon – important information if we are to stop young people becoming involved in knife crime.

Reflecting on his childhood in Baltimore, US writer Ta-Nehisi Coates said that 'when you live around violence, there is no opting out'. As a violence researcher, I spend much of my day thinking about why people become involved in violence and, in particular, why someone might carry a weapon. Coates's words, as relevant to England today as they are to 1980s Baltimore, are never far from my mind. They eloquently remind us that while violence and weapon-carrying may be individual decisions, these choices are not made in a vacuum.

Although weapon-carrying is rare – around 4% of young people in England and Wales carry a weapon once or more in a year – they contribute a great deal to the overall harm caused by violence. While around 15% of all violent incidents involve a weapon, more than half of all homicides do. Even when violence is not fatal, the harm weapons cause can have a significant emotional and psychological impact on the victim.

A study from 2019 showed that a history of violence, low trust in the police, drug use and criminal peers are common in young weapon carriers. However, because that study used data collected at a single point in time, it could not tell us what came first. For example, did violence lead to weapon-carrying? Or did carrying a weapon make them more likely to be violent? Similar questions about drug use, trust in the police and having friends in trouble with the police were also left unanswered.

The UK government's *Offending, Crime and Justice survey* was a survey of around 4,000 young people (ten to 25 years old) that asked about their experience of crime and the police at two points in time, about a year apart. The survey was conducted between 2003 and 2006, but remarkably, it is still the best data to understand the paths to knife crime for young people in England and Wales. Using it, we can now better understand the order of these experiences.

Because the researchers spoke to the same people twice, I was able to identify the people who started to carry a weapon sometime between the first and second surveys. I examined what these respondents said about their lives in the first year of the survey and compared their experiences and attitudes with those of young people who did not carry a weapon at all.

Life as a weapon-carrier

The first and most compelling finding was that for every violent incident a young person was involved in in the first year, the chance that they would carry a weapon the following year increased by about 6%. This was not just violence as a perpetrator, but also as a victim.

My research also found that, in the year before carrying a weapon, weapon-carriers were no more or less worried about being a victim than anyone else. This does not mean people involved in violence are not concerned about victimisation – they have repeatedly said they are – but it does suggest that this concern is not a direct cause of their weapon-carrying over a significant length of time. Maybe this is not surprising: the lives of young people can change quickly and a year between surveys may be too long to pick this up.

Whether or not someone carried a weapon was strongly connected to their peers. Having friends in trouble with the police was rare – 20% of people in the survey had a few such friends and only 1% had a lot – the more of their friends who were in trouble, the more likely that person was to carry a weapon in the following year.

There are many possible explanations for this. In adolescence, young people seem to value the opinions of their peers over anyone else. Their decisions about risky behaviour are unduly influenced by peers, as opposed to parents or other authority figures. Research from the US shows that when one friend in a group begins carrying a weapon, the likelihood that other members of the group will start carrying a weapon rises dramatically.

Although we talk about 'knife crime' as some distinct form of violence that has its own solutions, the truth is that weapon-carrying is the continuation of a long path paved with violence. For young people who live around violence, the decisions faced are often brutal and deeply unfair – and as Coates reminds us, there is no opting out. However, by identifying and tackling the early indicators, we can make violence preventable.

17 May 2022

THE CONVERSATION

The above information is reprinted with kind permission from The Conversation.
© 2010-2023, The Conversation Trust (UK) Limited

www.theconversation.com

#LifeorKnife - the consequences

Knife crime can lead to yourself or someone else being seriously injured or even killed. However, the effects of knife crime can be far more widespread. Someone doesn't even have to be injured!

Getting caught or committing a serious crime

You can receive a four-year prison sentence just for carrying a weapon, and that's without even intending to use it.

You can receive a permanent criminal record, and if you hurt someone you could go to prison for even longer.

Carrying a knife for protection is not a valid reason for the police. It actually means you're 51 per cent more likely to have it used against you.

Getting hurt

There's no safe place to get stabbed. If you get stabbed in the heart, you can lose all of your blood in one minute. A wound in the arm or the leg can still kill, and people have died from wounds to the leg because of severed arteries.

Knife crime isn't just life or death, you could be seriously injured as a result of being stabbed. This may mean you have a life changing disability or it could impact how you live the rest of your life.

Knife crime can have a negative mental impact. You don't have to be involved in a specific incident to be affected, from feeling on edge when you're out to suffering long-term trauma.

The people you care about

It doesn't matter if you are a victim or the offender, your loved ones are always going to be affected as a result of knife crime.

Loss is loss, and many families are devastated by losing someone they love whether that's because they can't see you because you're in prison or they have lost you completely through murder.

Your brothers and sisters will grow up without you being around and may face lots of questions at school. They may even be influenced by your actions, and follow in your footsteps.

Knife crime damages friendships and can damage your family's reputation with their friends and the local community.

Your lifestyle

Having a criminal record can even affect your social life. Many countries such as the USA and Australia are really strict about who they let in, even just for a holiday.

Your record may mean you might never be able to live or visit there.

Your future

A criminal record is permanent. When you apply for jobs and on many applications, you will always need to declare if you have a criminal record.

You will always have to declare your criminal record and complete enhanced DBS checks when applying for jobs in education, banks, armed forces, travel. If you want to get a taxi licence or private vehicle hire licence, you will have to declare your criminal record.

It will make it harder for you to get into college or university, and might mean you won't be able to go to the one you always wanted. This makes it much harder to find work, and it may affect your future career goals

Some jobs don't allow having a criminal record at all and will refuse your application.

An ex-gang member's message to YOU

Omar Sharif was just 13 years old when he started carrying a knife, he joined a gang and they became his new 'family'

When his friend Jevonne was stabbed and killed, he knew things had to change. He left London and moved to Coventry to get away from the gang and turn his life around.

He knows it's not easy to leave a gang and change your friends, but he learnt the hard way that when you need them most – your gang's not really there for you.

Activity

Create a poster to display some of the consequences of knife crime. Use #LifeorKnife for the title of your poster.

The above information is reprinted with kind permission from West Midlands Police.
© 2023 West Midlands Police

www.lifeorknife.west-midlands.police.uk

Lives not knives: young people's perspective on knife crime

An extract.

Young people's views: in brief

The young people we spoke to told us:

- Most knew of at least one person in their family, friendship group or local community who had been a victim of knife crime, some had been victims themselves
- Young people carry knives for a number of reasons: fear is the major driving factor, but people also carry knives to gain/maintain status, as a consequence of drug dealing and involvement in gangs
- Harsher penalties would not stop people carrying knives. There was little knowledge about the level of punishment for knife crimes, and fear and self-preservation were seen as more important
- They felt that the police did not protect them
- Knife crime is a problem that cannot be solved in isolation, action needs to focus on poverty and lack of opportunity too
- There were mixed views as to the effectiveness of increased stop and search
- All of the groups reported that it was very easy to buy knives and that more action should be taken to prevent knife sales to children

Young people's views: in detail

What experience of knife crime do the young people we spoke to have?

All of the participants in our focus groups were clear that the amount of knife crime in their local area had significantly increased in the last few years. They were also clear that young people were more likely to carry knives and commit knife crime than previously, but that it was not just young people that were involved.

> **'Loads are carrying, and not just teenagers.'** — Nacro learner

It was felt that it was mainly men and boys that carry knives, but not exclusively so, and that women and girls may be asked to carry weapons on behalf of others, as they are less likely to be stopped or searched by the police. All of the focus groups voiced their concern that violent crime in general had increased, not just knife crime. It was felt that people were increasingly using other weapons, such as bottles, and this also included guns.

Many of the participants in all of the focus groups knew of at least one person in their family, friendship group or local community who had been a victim of knife crime. The victims were generally of a similar age to the participants, but some also knew of older victims. Young victims of crime felt they were often treated with suspicion by the police.

Why do young people carry knives?

The views as to why young people were carrying knives varied to some extent from Centre to Centre:

- 'Eat or be eaten': All of the focus groups said that fear was a motivating factor, but to different extents. Fear was the first response to the question as to why people were carrying knives from one group. They said that if people were carrying knives out of fear then the risks of being caught with a knife by the police, or the threat of harsher punishments would not work to discourage them from carrying knives.
- 'They think they're the big man': One group felt that the primary motive was to gain status among friends and rivals.
- They also believed that it was related to gangs, and that in recent years there had been a migration of gang members from London and other cities.
- County lines drug trafficking was also said to be a cause in two of the groups, but views on this were more mixed elsewhere. Some told us that younger children are asked to commit crime (such as selling drugs) in return for payment. They felt that this was particularly the case for vulnerable children who were isolated or had no positive role models, who are then targeted with promises of love and friendship. The 'elders' in gangs protect themselves from getting arrested by getting the 'youngers' to do their dirty work. They told us that lots of people carry knives to protect themselves when they are carrying or dealing drugs.
- Postcode rivalry was no longer seen to be a motivating factor in one group, but this was still thought to be a significant factor in other locations.

An essential part of establishing 'what works' in terms of reducing knife crime involves understanding why people are carrying knives in the first place. Educational interventions should take into account one of the main reasons for carrying a knife: fear and the belief that carrying a knife provides protection. However, the effectiveness of education will be undermined if it is not supported by a much wider effort to enhance safety and reduce the vulnerability of young people in their communities. Criminal justice approaches, such as harsher penalties, concentrate on discouraging knife carrying by those people who carry in order to establish or maintain status, but this does not address fear as a driver of knife-carrying. Harsher penalties are unlikely to be effective with young people whose fear is not overridden by their knowledge and understanding of the potential consequences.

Young people's attitudes towards the police

'If the police don't protect you then you have to protect yourself': at one group we discussed the role that the police

could play in reducing fear among young people. Their perception was that the police can be heavy-handed with young people (for example showing up when they were just being a bit loud) and had negative and stereotyped views, but were then slow to react when there was a serious threat of violence against young people. We talked about when the learners might call the police if they were the victim of crime or threatened with violence, but they could not see any situation when they would do so. At another group, all participants were in agreement that the police were not interested when a young person was stabbed and would take more of an interest if an older person was stabbed, because if a young person was stabbed, they believed the police would assume that the victim was not entirely blameless. None of the focus groups said they would ever report an incident to the police.

'Snitches get stitches.' — Nacro learner

Some thought that if people felt under threat they would be likely to carry a knife in order to protect themselves. They felt that they would rather 'do time' than be injured or killed. Only one of the male participants in one group said he would not carry a knife if he were under threat, and he was clear that he knew the risks involved in carrying a knife and would not be willing to take those risks.

Whilst we know there are good examples of work done to build positive relationships between the police, young people and their local communities, we would suggest that in some areas there is much more work needed. We are concerned that increased use of stop and search has the potential to create further tension between the police, young people and the most vulnerable people that they serve.

What we do

We proactively engage with local police and other agencies, and have a role to play within Nacro Education Centres in facilitating dialogue and building relationships between our learners and the local police. Education Centre staff liaise with their local police on local issues, and facilitate sessions for our learners run by the police on a variety of issues, such as knife crime and county lines.

What is the role (and responsibility) of the media?

One group talked about *Grand Theft Auto* and how in that game you can stab people or hit them with baseball bats. They were unsure as to whether this would make some people more likely to stab someone themselves and did not think it made them act differently. We also talked about drill rappers and their lyrics. Some thought they rapped about criminal things that they had already done, but some thought that this was 'all talk'. They said this would not make them act differently but thought it could influence others to copy the behaviour. Some thought it was a good idea that drill rappers were being banned from YouTube, both because it removed the content but also because it made drill rappers clean up their act and behave more responsibly in order to be able to continue to promote themselves.

'It's not America': one group discussed how celebrities use social media to promote themselves, and post images of themselves with knives or guns. Some said these celebrities were American and young people did not copy that behaviour as our society was totally different, whereas others felt that young people in this country follow and try to emulate the culture that they see in America.

One participant said that there is a lot in the news about knife crime now. He said that 'white people are getting hurt and so it is seen as more relevant' and that is why it is in the news. He said people were not as interested when it was 'just' people from a BAME background. He said that news reporting 'advertises' knife crime and so it is part of the reason why people are more likely to carry knives. A participant in a different group described press reporting on the issue as 'propaganda'.

All of the groups that we spoke to are based outside London. They feel that the media is London-biased and that London news is broadcast across the country, and so people from all over the country think that knife crime is a problem in all areas. Conversely, it was felt that what is going on in places outside London does not get mentioned, which means that other areas of the country where it is an issue are being ignored.

We know that the evidence of a link between media violence and crime is weak, but it is important to note that the way people access violence in the media is constantly changing and so we would welcome ongoing evaluation of the potential link. In addition, research suggests that mass media can be used to reinforce the messages from school and community-based programmes on knife crime.

1 January 2020

The above information is reprinted with kind permission from Nacro.
© 2023 Nacro

www.nacro.org.uk

Chapter 2

Gangs & Violence

Gangs and street violence

The police define a gang as a group of people who are involved in organised crime activity.

A group of mates who live in the same area as each other, or all go to the same school, and who hang around together is not a gang and the police wouldn't see them as such as long as they were behaving in line with the law.

What is a gang?

The police define gangs as a group of people who may commit crimes or hurt people. They might carry knives or other weapons and use them either to show off or to threaten people. They might try to get you involved with them and what they do – or threaten to hurt you if you don't join them, or if you belong to another gang.

Gangs are often involved in various types of street crime, and being a victim of gang crime can happen to anyone. It could happen just to you, to other gangs or groups, or to whole communities. It often takes place in public areas such as on the street, in parks and shopping centres, and you may know the person or people committing the crime, or you may not.

There are many ways gang and street violence can be carried out:

- Antisocial behaviour (ASB): when other people's actions make you feel harassed, scared or unhappy.
- Stalking and harassment: when someone repeatedly follows you, watches you or spies on you.
- Intimidation through threats.
- Assault: when someone physically hurts you or threatens to physically hurt you.
- Hate crime: where people can be abusive to you or target you because of your identity, such as your race, religion, culture, gender identity, sexual orientation or disability.
- Theft: when your personal items are taken from you, including robbery.

I'm being pressured into joining a gang. What can I do?

It's important to remember that, although it may be hard sometimes, you don't have to do anything that you don't want to do. And no one has the right to force you into doing things that make you uncomfortable, or put you in danger.

It can be really difficult for children and young people to avoid being recruited or affected by gang activity, especially if it's in your neighbourhood. Being in a gang isn't a crime in itself, but it can put you at much greater risk of becoming a victim of crime, or an offender.

If your group of friends starts to get involved with gang activity, or any other activities you're uncomfortable with, think seriously about getting out. It's hard to leave behind the people you know, but there are lots of other people out there for you to make friends with, and lots of other activities you can get involved with that could be a lot safer. The most important thing is to keep yourself safe.

If you're worried because someone is trying to make you join a gang or become involved in activities that you're not comfortable with, you need to talk to an adult you can trust – such as a parent or family member, teacher, youth worker or support worker – about what's happening and how you feel about it. They will be able to help you.

Isn't it safer for me if I join a gang?

You might feel that if you join a gang you'll be looked after and protected, but often this is not true. Sometimes being in a gang makes you a target for people and you might find yourself in danger, particularly from other gangs.

Children and young people may also think that being in a gang will give them a glamorous lifestyle, but the reality is very different. As well as putting you at greater risk of being a victim of violence, being in a gang can also put you at greater risk of committing crime, dealing or taking drugs, and ending up in prison.

I'm being threatened, targeted or assaulted by a gang. What can I do?

It can be extremely frightening to be the victim of a gang. As well as possibly being hurt or injured physically, you can be very seriously affected emotionally. Many people find it hard to deal with the feeling of being powerless when someone is threatening them. Other common feelings include finding it hard to believe what has happened, feeling like your life is completely out of control, feeling angry towards those hurting you, and having physical symptoms such as 'the shakes', sleeplessness or crying all the time.

These reactions and many more are completely normal responses to being a victim of gang threats or violence. The important thing to remember is that it's not your fault – you haven't done anything wrong, and no one has the right to hurt or threaten you.

It can be even more frightening or worrying if you feel like you are trying to cope with what has happened on your own. Many young people find that it helps if they can talk to someone, and some things you can do are:

Tell an adult you trust. This could be a teacher, a family member, your youth worker or support worker. Tell them what's happened, and ask for their help and advice.

Think about reporting it to the police. If you think you are at immediate risk of getting hurt, call 999.

If you're worried or feel unsafe because of what's happened, talk to your trusted adult about developing a safety plan that would help you choose how best to keep yourself safe in the future.

Write down what has happened soon after the event including times and dates.

If you are worried about a friend, we have some tips on how you can start the conversation and get them the right help

Who can help me?

- Victim Support/You & Co – you can contact your nearest Victim Support office, call the 24/7 Supportline, contact us via live chat, or if you are 16 or older, you can create a My Support Space account. This is a free, safe and secure online space where you can work through interactive guides to help you move forward after crime.

- Childline – 24-hour support for young people, both on the phone and through online chats and message boards, on crime, safety and a range of other issues: 0800 1111.

- The Mix – information and support for under 25s on a whole range of issues. Get confidential help by email, text, webchat or phone: 0808 808 4994.

- Crimestoppers – if you want to provide information about a crime without talking to the police, you can contact Crimestoppers anonymously on 0800 555 111.

- Gangsline – for free advice and support from ex-gang members: 01375 483 239 or 07753 351 256.

The above information is reprinted with kind permission from Victim Support.
© 2023 Victim Support

www.victimsupport.org.uk

Scouse Soldiers: why do young people get involved in gangs?

An article from The Conversation.

By Robert Hesketh, Lecturer in Policing Studies, School of Justice Studies., Liverpool John Moores University

Like many urban areas in the UK, Merseyside has a long and notorious history of street gangs. From the Cornermen and High Rip gangs of the 19th century, to the Croxteth Crew, Nogga Dogs and Moss Edz, the self-perceived North Face 'Scouse Soldiers' of today, all have left a dark and deadly legacy.

As someone who has always lived on a former Merseyside council housing estate in Knowsley, one of the most socially excluded and poverty-stricken areas in the UK, and an academic whose research has focused on youth and gang crime, I have seen both sides of the fence. This experience has motivated me to research gangs on Merseyside – one of the UK's hot spots for gang and organised crime activity.

In 2018-19, social services assessed 16,132 children in Merseyside County, of which 546 were deemed to be either active members of a gang, at risk of joining one, or at risk of being a victim of gang-related violence.

Social networks

In 2009, sociologist Hannah Smithson and colleagues examined the extent, nature and causes of young people's involvement in gang and gun crime. From interviews with Merseyside police, practitioners and young people aged between 16 and 29, they identified two types of gang structures.

The first, a loosely-knit, non-hierarchical group of young people who would get together on the streets at night and engage in antisocial behaviour and potentially violence and criminality. This is the classic, stereotypical assumption of what a street gang is. The second type was structured and hierarchical, with ties to illegal drug markets and cities' adult organised crime groups.

In more recent years, these drug-dealing groups have become fiercely territorial and violent, resorting to the use of knives and firearms in order to protect their selling patch, and exploiting vulnerable young people.

Why do people get involved in gangs? I've sought to answer this key question in my own research, and found that a sense of belonging, respect and protection as well as membership as a source of income all contribute.

In 2018 I interviewed 44 young men – half involved in street gangs and half completely abstaining – to learn why some young people joined gangs. Social exclusion, coupled with cutbacks brought in by austerity policies, meant many young men who became involved in street gangs suffered from 'network poverty'. This means that they lacked the ability to make good 'pro-social' connections, which shape how young people perceive the welfare of others and their communities.

With friendships mainly restricted to the schoolyard or the residential streets, criminality is seen as a way to succeed in a world which values the ownership of material things. In the case of gang members, values become bound around deviant group formation and offending as a way of escape from continuing poverty and deprivation.

In contrast, young men who found opportunities beyond their local area abstained from gang affiliation and criminality. They joined interest groups such as martial arts classes or took weekend jobs, forging new friendships with peers away from their home streets. Their belief systems opened up, and they embraced legitimate employment and leisure activities, leading to further opportunities.

Deviant entrepreneurship

For those involved in street gangs, there was also the appeal of edgework – as risk-taking behaviour is described in criminology – which provided excitement and escapism

from the boredom and routine existence that social exclusion brings. Quite simply, there were no real legitimate opportunities for young people to access. Such thrill-seeking behaviour has not been adequately addressed by interventions aimed at countering gang recruitment.

In the eyes of many gang-involved young people, the line between employment and criminality (specifically drug dealing) became blurred. This was evident in interviews with gang members living closer to Liverpool city centre and its vibrant nighttime economy. Here, the language used during interviews became more businesslike – one participant identified his group as a 'firm of boys' and talked about serving punters (customers) and profit margins.

I coined the term 'deviant entrepreneurship' to describe the process of gangs making money through illegitimate means. Those gang members involved neutralised their criminal activity into the context of work, or as it is widely known on the streets around Liverpool, 'grafting'.

Across Merseyside, many young people involved in street gangs have become embroiled with adult organised crime groups as part of the 'county lines' phenomenon – a form of exploitation in which gangs of adults coerce children and young people to carry drugs to rural or coastal areas of the country.

In 2018, modern slavery researcher Grace Robinson interviewed a combination of young people (aged 14-20) and people working in youth justice interventions. Her research focused on exploitation within gangs by adult criminals. She found that some young people were paid a commission in drugs (in most cases, cannabis) in return for selling a supply.

Moreover, she identified the widespread use of social media platforms to lure young people into carrying out drug supplying tasks, and to manipulate them through debt bondage. Gang members offer young individuals trainers, designer clothes and sometimes even a place to stay or drugs for personal use. The young person is then forced into working to pay off the debt, by carrying drugs or recruiting other young people into the network, continuing the cycle of exploitation.

The existing research makes clear that gang activity on Merseyside is a major and continuing problem, and that addressing individualised symptoms alone will not stop young people becoming involved. A substantial part of this is the environment and lack of opportunities – something that should be addressed further by politicians.

Continuation of austerity policies, including cuts to youth services, coupled with unemployment and the financial consequences of the pandemic, have created socially deprived breeding grounds for street gangs and organised crime groups to flourish.

22 September 2021

THE CONVERSATION

The above information is reprinted with kind permission from The Conversation.
© 2010-2023, The Conversation Trust (UK) Limited

www.theconversation.com

Up to one in five teenage boys say they or their friends have been offered work by drug gangs, survey finds

Nearly one in five (19%) UK teenage boys say they or their friends have been offered work by drug suppliers, a survey commissioned by British Transport Police (BTP) suggests.

Data further reveals that more than a quarter (27%) of boys aged 13 to 19 have seen drugs being offered or sold either at school or on social media.

To counter drug suppliers' attempts to groom, manipulate and seduce children into the drug trade, BTP has today (1 March) launched an all-new campaign. The 'Don't Take the Bait' digital campaign highlights the tactics drug gangs use to coerce and exploit teens.

Drug gangs are known to offer money, mobile phones, gaming tokens, vapes and clothing in exchange for what they present as a 'business opportunity'. Social media messages sent by drug suppliers to teenagers seen by BTP include, 'who wants to make £500 this weekend?' and 'who wants overtime?'.

BTP's dedicated County Lines Taskforce routinely encounter young and vulnerable people on the railway who have been exploited by gangs to carry drugs between locations.

The force is urging parents to speak to their children about the tactics county lines drug gangs use to hook them into a life of fear, violence and scams.

Since the Taskforce was setup with Home Office funding in late 2019 to tackle county lines activity on the railway, it has made 2,250 arrests and thousands of vital safeguarding interventions, including 115 referrals into the national referral mechanism for safeguarding.

Of those arrested, 40 per cent have been under the age of 19, however, only one in five (20%) have been criminalised.

Detective Superintendent Gareth Williams, BTP's County Lines Taskforce lead, said: 'It's not uncommon for my dedicated teams to encounter children on the railway who are being exploited to traffic drugs.

'Supported by safeguarding experts, a key priority of ours is to identify these victims and pull them out of harm's way. The youngest person we've found being exploited in county lines activity was a boy aged 13 – in that case the couple controlling him to courier drugs were jailed for over 12 years.

'We're relentless in our pursuit of these heartless human traffickers, and we are utilising modern slavery legislation to ensure they serve adequately lengthy jail terms.'

> If you know who is exploiting young people in this way, you can give information 100% anonymously at fearless.org. Fearless are not the police, they are a charity. Anonymous means your identity is completely unknown.

1 March 2023

Key Facts
- 19% of teenage boys in the UK say that they or their friends have been offered work by drug suppliers.
- 27% of boys aged 13 to 19 have seen drugs being offered or sold either at school or on social media.
- since 2019 British Transport Police have made 2,250 arrests and thousands of safeguarding interventions.

The above information is reprinted with kind permission from the British Transport Police.
© 2023 British Transport Police

www.btp.police.uk

New figures reveal 12,720 children in England were at risk of criminal exploitation

New figures published this morning by the Department for Education reveal 12,720 children assessed by children's social services in England between 1 April 2020 and 31 March 2021 were deemed to be at risk due to gang involvement. The figures also show there were 16,830 children where child sexual exploitation was a factor during their assessment and 2,710 children where trafficking was a factor.

The overall statistics, in the DfE's annual Children in Need data, also reveal a fall in the number of children being referred to social services during the Covid pandemic lockdown. The figures show there was a 31% drop in referrals via schools during the period when schools were closed twice to most children. This suggests some vulnerable children did drop out of the sight of teachers, who are often the first to spot the need for children's social services to assess a child.

The Commission on Young Lives, the independent year-long commission looking at how to develop a national plan to divert vulnerable children away from gangs and serious violence chaired by former Children's Commissioner Anne Longfield, is warning that the number of children referred for gangs is likely to be the tip of the iceberg, with overall referrals falling over the last year during lockdown.

Today's statistics show:

- There were 496,030 episodes of a child being referred to social services in 2020/21 compared to 522,990 in 2019/20, a fall of 5%.
- The number of times a school made a referral to social services fell from 117,010 in pre-Covid 2019/20 to 81,180 in 2020/21 when there were two school lockdowns - a drop of 31%.
- There were 12,720 children identified by children's social services as at risk due to involvement in gangs in 2020/21. This is 13% lower than pre-Covid 2019/20 (14,700) but still 16% higher than 2018/19 (10,960).
- In London, 3,500 children were identified as a being at risk as a result of involvement with gangs, while 2,650 children were identified as being at risk as a result of child sexual exploitation.
- In the North West, 1,750 children were identified as a being at risk as a result of involvement with gangs while 2,440 were identified as being at risk as a result of child sexual exploitation.
- In Yorkshire and the Humber, 1,090 children were identified as being at risk as a result of involvement with gangs and 1,760 as a result of child sexual exploitation.
- In the South East, 1,510 children were identified as being at risk as a result of involvement with gangs and 2,540 were identified as being at risk as a result of child sexual exploitation.
- In the West Midlands, 1,550 children were identified as being at risk as a result of involvement with gangs and 1,910 children were identified as being at risk as a result of child sexual exploitation.
- In the East of England, 1,170 children were identified as being at risk as a result of involvement with gangs and 1,480 were identified as being at risk as a result of child sexual exploitation.

Anne Longfield, Chair of the Commission on Young Lives and former Children's Commissioner for England, responding to the figures, said:

'The number of children being referred to social services because of fears of gang exploitation is extremely troubling and likely only the tip of the iceberg. During a period when the country was in lockdown twice, thousands of vulnerable children were still being sucked into gangs, serious violence and crime or sexually exploited.

'I am particularly worried about the very sharp drop in referrals during the two school lockdowns. Even though schools were open for vulnerable children, many did not attend, and it is very concerning that many have dropped off the radar since.

'We need to ask why we are still losing thousands of marginalised teenagers to the ruthless criminals who are so adept at spotting and exploiting vulnerable children and how we can find better solutions to stop it from happening.

'It is clear these problems are not going to solve themselves and we are still giving too many abusers and exploiters a free pass to use and harm children.

'The systems that are supposed to be there to help vulnerable children are under pressure and badly need reforming. It is time to find new ways of bringing hope and success to young people who fall through the gaps and end up in danger.

'I welcome the announcements of funding for children and families in the Budget. But this needs to be the start of something much bigger to enable all children and young people to be part of this new era, and so that the most vulnerable children are given the same chances to level up as any other child.'

28 October 2021

The above information is reprinted with kind permission from Commission on Young Lives - Oasis UK.
© Oasis 2023

www.thecommissiononyounglives.co.uk

What is county lines?

County lines is not a new thing. You may have heard about it on the news or in TV shows like Hollyoaks. But beyond the headlines and scripts, it's a stark reality for many young people. Here we unpack the truth about county lines and how we work to restore the hopes of children being forced to carry drugs across the country.

What does county lines mean?

County lines is a form of criminal exploitation. It is when criminals befriend children, either online of offline, and then manipulate them into drug dealing. The 'lines' refer to mobile phones that are used to control a young person who is delivering drugs, often to towns outside their home county.

Here are some things you might not know about county lines exploitation:

Children as young as seven are targeted

Young people aged 14-17 are most likely to be targeted by criminal groups but there are reports of seven year olds being groomed into county lines.

Primary school children are seen as easy targets because they're less likely to get caught. The grooming might start with them being asked to 'keep watch' but it soon escalates to them being forced to stash weapons, money, or become drug couriers.

County lines is everywhere

Just because county lines may not get the coverage of other societal issues, it doesn't mean it's a small problem. In fact, most police forces across the country have reported county lines activity in their area and they say the violence is getting worse. It's not just a 'big city' problem. County lines is far reaching, with many smaller towns being affected.

> **County lines facts**
>
> 90% of English police forces have seen county lines activity in their area and the violence is getting worse.
>
> 4 in 5 parents are worried about county lines in their local area.

We work with children from London, Birmingham and Greater Manchester who have been trafficked all over the country to other big cities as well as smaller towns. We also work with professionals across various counties.

In Northumberland, our Prevention Team highlighted how easy it was to find the details of children in residential care. Exploiters could easily identify potential victims with a simple online search, putting many children at risk. This is now changing. Public information is being reviewed and more children are being safeguarded.

It affects all communities

It doesn't matter where you're from or your social background, children from any community can be groomed into county lines. However, those from poor households, who regularly skip school or have problems at home may be more at risk.

Our Next Generation service in Nottingham worked with three young people who had low attendance at school and were at risk of being exploited. After two years, their attendance is at 100%. They are more focused on their education and less likely to be targeted.

We also work with those who regularly go missing to escape problems at home. Again, this makes them a target for exploitation. The young people we worked with had 56 missing incidents between them at the start. They now only have two.

Children are not the problem

This may sound obvious but only recently has there been some recognition of the fact that a child caught up in county lines is a victim of exploitation. Often they are treated as criminals, not victims. Fortunately, attitudes are changing. However, gender, age, ethnicity and background can still affect how professionals respond to children.

We work hard so any child affected by county lines gets the support they need to escape a life of exploitation. We train police, social workers and other professionals so they can better respond to children and make them feel safe rather than criminalised.

County lines is visible

County lines operations are often hard to spot, but the signs are visible. We could all be in a position to stop it.

You might notice a child has multiple mobiles, comes home with unexplained injuries or bruising, suddenly has new trainers they can't afford. These could all be indicators that a young person is in trouble. We encourage everyone to learn the signs of exploitation and how to report it if worried.

Young people can and should live a life free of exploitation. Together we can help them break free from their abusers and face their future with confidence.

The above information is reprinted with kind permission from The Children's Society.
© The Children's Society 2023

www.childrenssociety.org.uk

County Lines: what is it and what can we do to tackle it?

'You good for Monday, yeah? I have paid for ya ticket and got you those trainers you wanted, remember you're going to this address and picking that package up, keep ya phone on, don't talk to anyone and you will be looked after, just remember don't mess this up.' As simple as that, this young person is now part of a county line.

What is County Lines?

A county line is a phone line used by a gang to coordinate drug dealing across the country, the term county line can also be reference to the phone line used or the geographical route between counties to distribute drugs.

How big is the problem and who is affected?

The most recent statistics from the National Crime Agency suggests there are more than 2,000 individual deal lines in the UK linked to approximately 1,000 branded county lines. According to figures from The Children's Society, 46,000 children in England are thought to be involved in gangs, 84% of parents are worried about county lines in their area and 4,000 teenagers are being criminally exploited in London alone.

All drugs in the UK distributed have more than likely passed through a county line. So what makes it different to drug importation and day to day drug dealing on the street? The difference is the long term coordination and logistical planning that is needed for a county line to work effectively. To do this you need numbers, you need people. And you need people that won't ask questions, people that want to be a part of something and people that need money. Unfortunately, the demographic that meets this criteria is the young and vulnerable of our country.

How do they recruit?

The recruitment side of things is as planned and coordinated as the county line itself, with perpetrators often using a number of means to reach the young and vulnerable. Social media platforms are being used by these gangs to target individuals, going as far as to post upmarket adverts with the tag line 'recruitment opportunities available'. These adverts normalise county lines, making them seem legitimate and acceptable – like a professional job advert.

If the perpetrators can normalise the action, they can manipulate and recruit young and vulnerable people.

Online gaming is also being used to reach young people, through private chats and reach young people who would not be reachable via social media. If the gang can create a safe environment for the young person to open up – and turn to them instead of peers and parents – then they can isolate and manipulate that person, more often than not leaving parents and carers unaware.

Once recruited, social media is used to coordinate individual details, promote deliveries and encourage violence towards other rival gangs. The key to any 'successful' county line is communication. And social media is an effective tool to do this, with fake online profiles created to protect the perpetrator's true identity.

What can we do to tackle County Lines?

Communication between statutory organisations, charities, professionals, social media and communities is imperative in protecting our young people from exploitation. We need communities to be aware of exploitation and indicators, to share information and intelligence with statutory organisations and to create safe spaces in the community for young people to access and seek help. We need social media platforms to be quick in shutting down accounts.

What can we do to protect our children?

Although often easier said than done, having a safe and open environment at home is probably the best way to minimise the risk of a child being criminally exploited. If a child feels safe and secure then they are more likely to talk about any unusual behaviour they encounter online and raise concerns before they're drawn into dangerous situations.

But we know that perpetrators are using increasingly sophisticated grooming techniques – and it's easy for anyone, no matter what their background, to be drawn in.

What we do know though, is that the cost of living crisis is exacerbating young people's vulnerability to this sort of abuse – as many feel compelled to earn money to support both their, and their families, standard of living.

To seriously reduce risks of exploitation and county lines we need everyone to be aware of the signs and indicators, to share information and therefore to bring perpetrators to justice. But we also we need to reduce vulnerability amongst our young people that makes them easier victims – which means support for the most hard hit families, good access to mental health services and far earlier intervention when we know a child or young person is struggling.

1 February 2023

The above information is reprinted with kind permission from Catch22.
© 2023 Catch22

www.catch-22.org.uk

'How I escaped a county lines drug gang'

Hundreds of children are recruited each year by brutal county lines gangs around Britain. Thanks to Action for Children, Jay found a way out.

By Joe Shute, senior feature writer

Christmas 2021, Jay* turned up on the doorstep of his family home, gaunt and dishevelled. The then 18-year-old, who has special educational needs, had disappeared for over a week, sent by a gang from his native north-east to sell drugs from a squalid address in a city in the Midlands.

'He looked terrible when he came back,' his mother, Elizabeth*, recalls. 'He wouldn't make eye contact or communicate. It was like the weight of the world was on his shoulders. It was horrific.'

This had been Jay's life for the previous two years after becoming embroiled in what is known as county lines, a tactic increasingly adopted by criminal gangs in which children are groomed and recruited to sell drugs nationwide. From the age of 16 he would slip out from the family home in the dead of night and disappear across the country for days, sometimes weeks, to sell large amounts of heroin, crack cocaine, ketamine, cocaine, MDMA and cannabis with a street value of thousands of pounds.

Generally he would pack little more than a spare tracksuit, plus a hammer and knife in his coat pocket for protection. He would be given a burner phone (one that is cheap and easy to discard) and stationed at an address belonging to a drug addict known as a 'trap house' to deal across the wider area. For the dealers at the top, it means the address and drugs cannot be traced back to them in the event of a police raid. All the risk is instead put on children like Jay.

Jay recalls one early trip down south. At the beginning, he says with a disarming, dimpled smile, 'it felt a bit like a holiday', marvelling at the grand buildings and bustle of London, a city he had never previously visited. Once he arrived, however, he was placed in a filthy flat with a crack addict for company.

There was no television, food, or even toilet roll. In between dealing, Jay stayed awake for days on end, afraid he would be attacked or robbed if he closed his eyes. Initially drawn in by expensive gifts and the prospect of high earnings, he soon realised that the reality was not as it had been depicted by older gang members. 'There were times I was really scared and you would never know what was going to happen. Everything was a risk.'

How gangs target vulnerable children

Ever more young people from across the country are becoming ensnared by county lines. According to Home Office figures, from July to September 2022, 577 people were referred as suspected victims of county lines exploitation. The vast majority were children – at least 479. Between April and June, the total was 601 – the highest quarterly figure ever recorded – with that number again overwhelmingly comprised of children.

But experts fear that these figures are merely the tip of the iceberg. In the year up to March 2021, 12,720 children in England were identified by social services as being at risk of criminal exploitation by gangs. Former children's commissioner Anne Longfield, who chairs the Commission on Young Lives, recently warned that while gangs previously targeted children in care or with vulnerable parents almost exclusively, they are increasingly recruiting middle-class children into county lines.

'More and more middle-class families are finding burner phones or large amounts of cash in their children's bedrooms and you can imagine their horror,' Longfield told The Yorkshire Post last March, stressing that 'this is happening all around the country'.

Following the publication of the Commission on Young Lives' final report in November, Longfield said children running drugs for gangs has become an 'epidemic'.

The tactics used to recruit young people, Jay explains, combine inveiglement and menace. 'They pretend like they are your friend and offer to buy you nice things but it's all a game to them,' he says.

He knows of young people stabbed as a result, or now in prison. 'The consequences are very serious. If you do stuff like that you are going to get caught, go to jail or worse.'

When we meet it is the run-up to Christmas, and we are sitting in Jay's mother's spotless living room. Elizabeth, 47, a former canteen worker, has dressed the tree and put out advent calendars for her four children, aged six to 17, who live with her. Jay now lives in supported accommodation nearby but often stays over to spend time with his mother and siblings. His father left the family when he was growing up.

Elizabeth beams at the prospect of their first settled Christmas together for years. On occasions when Jay stays at the family home, she still wakes and checks his room several times a night. 'It will be a long time before I stop that.'

Jay had been groomed by a gang on the estate where his family lived at the beginning of lockdown. Though he had struggled at school and left aged 16, he was a talented football player and relied on the discipline of training. The disruption of his normal routine, as a result of the pandemic, made him easy prey.

A recent report by the National Youth Agency into county lines activity found a trend of gangs increasingly targeting vulnerable young people during lockdown, and in particular using social media more to attract new recruits.

From happy homebody to withdrawn teen

Previously, Elizabeth explains, Jay was a 'homebody'. When not playing football he would happily stay in his bedroom, which he kept immaculate, messing around on the PlayStation. He would never miss a family meal.

Suddenly, though, he started roaming the streets with other teenagers from the estate. After being introduced to the gang 'elders' – a key aspect of county lines is that youngsters are instructed to groom other potential recruits – he was quickly coerced into drug dealing, and paid £500 for each week spent in a trap house, with his wages docked for food.

Elizabeth would plead with her son to stay at home, although often the ensuing argument resulted in Jay storming out. Whenever he went missing she reported his absence to the police, but she had little idea of the bleak world into which he had been pulled. 'I didn't even know about county lines and couldn't believe it when I first heard from the police,' she says. 'I told them, "Are we talking about the same kid?"'

Jay doesn't open up easily but as he describes some of his experiences, his mum gasps. 'I'm just so grateful he is here, has changed, is seeing things differently and knows these people aren't his friends,' she says.

One of the catalysts for that change is sitting on the sofa next to Jay: a 27-year-old woman called Marie*, his mentor.

About a year ago, Jay was referred by police to the Serious Organised Crime Early Intervention Service operated by Action for Children. The specialist service was the first of its kind in Europe when it launched in Glasgow in 2013, and has since been rolled out across Edinburgh, Dundee, Cardiff and the north-east. The project relies on 'peer mentors' who have similar backgrounds to the young people they support.

The mentors, some of whom are ex-young offenders and are head-hunted for the role, are matched with 11- to 18-year-olds and provide a source of support and advice. 'Marie has changed my life, to be honest,' Jay says.

The service is kept low-key by Action for Children, one of four charities supported by this year's Telegraph Christmas appeal. County lines gangs often try to lure people back into the fold, and strict anonymity is enshrined for both service users and mentors. The service operates in partnership with a range of organisations, including social workers and the police. If a young person tells a mentor they have committed a serious crime, they are obliged to contact the police in the interests of child protection, but otherwise the relationship is confidential.

Since he was referred to the service, Jay's family have been moved off the estate where they lived to a secure address. He has changed his phone number several times. Gang members still attempt to contact him via his Snapchat and Instagram accounts, which he keeps open to stay in touch with friends.

Sometimes it will be an offer of a meal, or a drink. On one occasion, when the family still lived at their previous home, they threatened to burn it down if he didn't start dealing again.

The Serious Organised Crime Early Intervention Service has already achieved success. According to one analysis conducted between 2013 and 2019, two thirds of teenagers the Glasgow team worked with had 'significantly improved' offending behaviour. One teenager who had committed almost 600 offences ceased all criminal activity after becoming involved.

A trial with Glasgow City Council found that the service demonstrated £500,000 savings over six months by diverting just four youngsters deemed 'high risk' away from secure care. According to Ministry of Justice figures, it costs on average more than £270,000 a year to keep a child in youth custody in a secure children's home; £119,000 in a young offenders institution.

Of the 181 children and young people the service worked with nationwide between 2018 and 2021, 83 per cent have reduced offending behaviour and 67 per cent improved engagement in school. In total over the past year, 65 per cent of young participants previously involved with serious organised crime were deemed no longer at risk of exploitation.

Paul Carberry, Action for Children's director for Scotland and a member of the Scottish Government's Serious Organised Crime Taskforce, has been involved with the service since its inception. He has worked in youth criminal justice for 35 years, inspired by his own childhood in Glasgow's Govan district. 'When I grew up you saw lots of children who went down a particular road because they had no other choices,' he says. 'They didn't achieve, no matter how bright they were, but with the right support they could have done anything with their lives.'

Carberry also recalls several recent incidents of children from families with professional backgrounds who have been involved in county lines, and seriously exploited and harmed. 'These are families who never in their wildest dreams thought their children would be travelling from Scotland to London and being involved with organised crime groups.'

The majority of children they work with are between 14 and 18, but increasingly, he warns, gangs can pounce at any time. Recently, Marie started supporting a 13-year-old who was discovered slipping out of school each morning to sell drugs from an abandoned car before returning at the end of the day to take the bus home.

Becoming a mentor

Like Jay, Marie grew up on a council estate in the north-east with a big family (four siblings in her case) and a father who was largely absent (working on oil rigs for long periods). Her mother had always been a heavy drinker but spiralled into chronic alcoholism when Marie was nine, drinking up to a litre and a half of vodka a day. It was down to Marie to raise her then two-year-old sister and look after her mother.

'I used to dress her and get her up off the floor when she couldn't walk,' she recalls. On one occasion her mother tripped backwards down the stairs, smashing her head on a windowsill and suffering a heavy bleed on the brain. Aged 13, Marie had to put her sister to bed and call an ambulance. She says her mother nearly died.

'She was quite an aggressive drunk and when she had been out drinking would come home full of rage,' Marie adds. 'She would use vile words and I couldn't tell you a time when she told us she loved us… She was very heavy-handed with us.'

When she was 15, marks were spotted on Marie's back in the school changing rooms and she and her sister were referred to social services, then sent to live with an aunt. Remarkably, she achieved 13 GCSEs and read psychology at Teesside University, before completing a Master's in criminology. Her sister is currently at university and they remain in touch with their mother, who has curbed her drinking.

Marie credits her recovery from the trauma of her childhood to a mentor she was assigned through a north-east drugs and alcohol support service when she was 15. 'The first three sessions I didn't speak a word because I was worried I would say something wrong,' she says. 'But she became a second parent to me.'

That mentor helped her make it through school and university, and when Marie, who is engaged, gets married, she will be a guest at the wedding. They meet for a coffee each week, and the mentor first alerted Marie to the opportunity to work for the Serious Organised Crime Early Intervention Service – a paid, full-time role. 'If I can be half the person she was to me growing up then I am doing good in my job,' Marie says.

Although Marie never became embroiled in county lines herself, many of Action for Children's peer mentors were groomed into a life of crime from a young age before turning things around. They now use their own experiences to help vulnerable children like Jay.

He, too, has started to pass on the lessons he has learned to younger people – and he knows a criminal record would jeopardise that. He is also currently working in a gym, helping teach classes to children. 'Now I feel I'm on the right track, I don't want to ruin that opportunity.'

Yet the ghosts of his recent past cluster close by. When walking on the street he is constantly looking over his shoulder. Though he is not in contact with the gangs, his phone, which buzzes with messages from friends while we speak, can quickly offer a portal into the world he has escaped. According to Marie, it can take only days for a young person to be lured back.

But Jay is firm that his life has turned around. 'I've had to grow up quickly and it has taught me a lot,' he says. 'Having family and people that care around you is the most important thing.'

*Names have been changed

9 January 2023

The above information is reprinted with kind permission from *The Telegraph*.
© Telegraph Media Group Limited 2023

www.telegraph.co.uk

Girls in gangs: how they are recruited, exploited and trapped

An article from The Conversation.

By Tirion Havard, Associate Professor of Social Work, London South Bank University

There has long been a misconception that gangs are made up of boys and young men, typically from ethnic minority groups and disadvantaged backgrounds. But the reality is very different.

Girls and young women from all demographics are targeted by gang members, and used to transport drugs and weapons from urban areas to rural locations and coastal towns.

Research in London's Waltham Forest in 2018 found that 'clean skins' – children, especially young women and girls, not previously known to police and statutory agencies and often from wealthier backgrounds – are being targeted by gangs.

When young women and girls are recognised as part of gangs, they tend to be viewed as willing participants, and judged according to sexist social norms and stereotypes. Their behaviours are interpreted as one of two extremes: they are either very violent, or immoral and sexually promiscuous. For example, so-called hooks or honey traps are commonly seen as perpetrators, willingly manipulating their sexuality to entice rival gang members or attract new ones.

The truth is far more complex. Women and girls involved in gangs are often both perpetrator and victim, actively recruiting other young people to avoid their own sexual and criminal exploitation.

The limited public awareness of girls and young women in gangs is to the gang's advantage. Absent from the statistics and viewed as deviant, they are seldom seen and less often believed, which means they can more readily avoid detection. In this sense, girls and young women from diverse backgrounds are ideally placed to help gangs run their profit making business model.

Challenging these conceptions and improving public understanding about girls in gangs could help prevent more young women from being recruited and used to perpetuate criminal activity.

Coercive control

A better way to understand the behaviour of girls and young women in gangs is the concept of coercive control. Historically associated with domestic abuse, coercive control is built on a foundation of trust, where the victim shares intimate experiences and information with the perpetrator, including personal dreams and fears. It is different from other forms of abuse, because abusers leverage the privileged and trusted information to exert influence or control over their victim.

The BBC documentary *Hidden Girls*, which I consulted on, describes first-hand accounts of the ways girls are recruited into gangs. Young men in gangs show an interest in or feign concern about young women and girls. They target these children and deliberately foster a dependency which leads to an emotional commitment.

In the hands of gang members, technology becomes a tool for coercive control. Gang members regularly use social media to recruit young women and girls from all backgrounds to parties. Here, they are plied with drink and drugs and sexually exploited, often by several gang members at a time. They are often too drunk to give consent or too frightened to say no, and the rape is filmed. Armed with evidence of the girl or young woman's alleged promiscuity, gang members then threaten to expose them by posting the footage and their personal information on social media. These young women and girls are then bombarded with sexually explicit texts and phone calls from predatory strangers.

Technology can also be used to groom young women and girls by creating the impression of a romantic relationship. Once in the gang fold, this same technology is used to intimidate and maintain round the clock surveillance. Equipped with their personal numbers, elder gang members are able to track young women and girls through GPS apps on their phones.

Always knowing where they are and able to text or call at any time, gang members can make demands at a moment's notice, while monitoring the girls to check on their whereabouts and ensure they are following instructions. This creates the impression that the perpetrator is always present, even when he cannot be seen. This fear traps the girls in gang life and forces them to comply with the demands of gang members.

Gangs are targeting young women and girls from all backgrounds. The myths and stereotypes associated with gang demographics only serve to isolate these women and girls and keep them hidden. We need to recognise that all children are vulnerable to recruitment and that their decisions, however unwise, may be a consequence of fear and control. Rather than judge these young women and girls, it may be helpful to understand their behaviours as a strategy to manage their abuse and a tool to keep themselves safe.

17 February 2022

THE CONVERSATION

The above information is reprinted with kind permission from The Conversation.
© 2010-2023, The Conversation Trust (UK) Limited

www.theconversation.com

Tackling Youth Crime

Chapter 3

Stop and search

What are 'reasonable grounds' for a stop and search? What's the difference between a suspicion-based and a suspicionless stop and search? What are my rights?

'Stop and search' are the powers the police have to stop people in order to search them. It's one of the most controversial and most criticised police powers. The police's stop and search powers are often used incorrectly or unfairly. People feel like they've been stopped for no reason – and they're not sure of their rights. Liberty has criticised the government for its racist and discriminatory use of stop and search.

What is 'stop and search'?

This page gives you information on the two main types of stop and search powers:

1. Suspicion-based stop and search
2. Suspicion-less stop and search

We have also included some information on stop and search for people under Serious Violence Reduction Orders (SVROs).

1. Suspicion-based stop and search

This is when the police stop you and they have a genuine reason to suspect you are carrying something illegal. For example

- drugs
- a weapon
- stolen property
- something that could be used to commit a crime.

This genuine suspicion must be based on reasonable grounds.

What does 'reasonable grounds' mean?

The College of Policing is a professional body for police staff. Their guide on fairness in stop and search says 'reasonable grounds' means that:

- The officer must genuinely suspect that they will find the item they're searching for. This suspicion should be about how likely it is that you have the item. It shouldn't be based on how likely they think it is that you're breaking the law.

- It must be objectively reasonable for them to suspect this, given the information they had. This means that it is what an ordinary person would think was fair if they had all the information the police officer has.

Unless the police have information which provides a description of someone carrying an illegal item, the reasonable grounds cannot be based on

- your physical appearance
- being part of a category of people, such as being a black girl, or
- generalisations or stereotypes.

In some cases, the police can stop you because of your behaviour or because of where you are at a certain time. If the police believe you are acting suspiciously, they must be able to explain how your behaviour was suspicious.

A hunch or a 'vibe' does not count as reasonable grounds unless it can be fully explained to another neutral person who was observing in a way that would allow them to reach the same conclusion.

If the police have no reasonable grounds, you are free to leave, and the police should tell you this.

You have the right to know the grounds for the search

- when you're being searched
- on the record of the search, if you ask for it

2. Suspicionless stop and search

Section 60 searches

Section 60 of the Criminal Justice and Public Order Act 1994 allows a police officer to stop and search a person without suspicion. These searches are known as Section 60 searches.

This is different from ordinary 'stop and search' because it means the police don't need to have 'reasonable grounds' in order to stop and search you.

Who can authorise a Section 60 search?

Section 60 searches can only be carried out if a senior police officer authorises them. This senior police officer must be at least the rank of Inspector.

To authorise Section 60 'stop and searches', the senior police officer must reasonably believe that:

- Incidents involving serious violence may take place in the officer's area – and authorisation will help to prevent them, OR
- An incident involving serious violence has taken place in the officer's area and that a weapon used in the incident is being carried in the area – and authorisation will help to find the weapon, OR
- People are carrying weapons in the officer's area without good reason.

If a Section 60 authorisation has been granted, there is little you can do to prevent the police carrying out this type of stop and search.

How long can the authorisation last?

The authorisation usually lasts for 24 hours – although it can sometimes be extended.

Searches for people under serious violence reduction orders

Serious Violence Reduction Orders (SVROs) were introduced under the new Policing Act. The Policing Act is officially called the Police, Crime, Sentencing and Courts Act 2022 (PCSC Act).

The key thing is that if you have an SVRO made against you, the police can stop and search you to find out if you're carrying a bladed article. If you are in a public place, the police don't need to have reasonable suspicion to do this.

To stop and search you under these powers, the police should ensure that you are subject to an SVRO.

If an officer is unsure of your identity, they should

- try to find out your identity
- check to see if you have an SVRO before they search you. They can do this by looking it up on the Police National Computer. The PNC is a national database of information available to all UK police forces.

If a police officer can't confirm that you are subject to an SVRO, they can't search you unless

- they have reasonable suspicion under their usual stop and search powers, or
- other stop and search powers apply, such as a section 60 authorisation.

If they don't have other grounds to search you, but search you anyway, the Government guidance says the search will be unlawful.

What are my rights if I'm stopped and searched?

The College of Policing have a guide on how police should behave when they stop and search people. It says that the police must search you in accordance with GOWISELY.

What's GOWISELY?

It's an acronym – each letter of GOWISELY stands for your rights if you're stopped and searched.

G: Grounds for suspicion. For suspicion based searches, the police should tell you why they suspect that you might be carrying something illegal. This could be information they have, or something they noticed you doing (your behaviour). For Section 60 searches, the police should tell you that the search was authorised under those powers.

O: object of the search. The police should clearly explain what they are looking for.

W: warrant card. The police should give you this if you ask for it, or if they aren't wearing a uniform.

I: identity of the police officer or officers. The police officers involved in stopping and searching you should give you their name and number. They only have to give you their warrant and collar number if the case involves terrorism, or if there is a specific risk to the officer.

S: station. The police should tell you which police station they work with.

E: entitlement. The police should tell you that you have the right to have a copy of the search record within 3 months.

L: legal power used. The police should tell you what legal power they are using to stop and search you.

Y: you are detained for the purposes of a search. The police should tell you that you are being detained because they will search you. Detained means being stopped by the police and not being free to leave until they tell you so.

Key things to remember

If the police stop and search you, they must:

- give their name and police station
- tell you what they expect to find
- explain the reasons for the search
- make a record of the search – unless it's not practical to do so.

How long can police keep me for?

They can only detain you during the search – and only for as short a time as possible.

If they don't have reasonable grounds, the search is unlawful and so is keeping you there. If so, you could take legal action or make a complaint against the police.

Can I get a record of the search?

If the police stop and search you, they should tell you that you have the right to a copy of any record of the search. You can get the record if you ask within 3 months of the search.

If you are not arrested and taken to a police station, you can get the record immediately after they finish searching you. However, the police don't have to do this if they are called away to a higher priority incident.

If they don't give you one straight away, the police should give you information on how you can get a copy. This can be in the form of a small business card.

These records are important if you want to complain about the search.

Do the police always make a record of the search?

Normally, the police must make a record of the search.

This record can be made electronically or on paper. However, they don't have to do this if it is not feasible.

This record must include certain details such as:

- Your ethnicity
- The date, time and place of the search
- What the police were looking for
- The identity of all officers involved in the search

For Section 60 searches: the record should give details of the authorisation. You also have the right to a written statement that you have been stopped and searched under section 60 if you apply within 1 year.

For searches based on suspicion: the record must include the reasonable grounds for suspicion.

The record does not have to include your name, address or date of birth.

Full requirements for recording stop and searches are found in Section 4 of PACE Code A.

> ### Design
> Create a poster to display the GOWISELY rights for stop and search.

Can they strip search me?

They can ask you to take off your outer coat, jacket and gloves. Anything more and they must take you to a police station – or out of public view to a police tent.

They can't use force to remove your clothes, as this could be assault.

If they don't take reasonable steps to comply with these rules, the search may be considered unlawful.

Treating people fairly

When they stop and search someone, the police still have to do it fairly and respect the person's rights under the Equality Act 2010. They should not stop and search you because of things like your:

- race (including nationality and ethnic background)
- age
- sex
- sexual orientation
- gender reassignment
- disability
- religion or faith.

Standing up for your rights

If you feel you have been stopped for no good reason or have been treated unfairly, you can make a police complaint. If you have been arrested and charged, we advise you to get help from a solicitor.

The above information is reprinted with kind permission from Liberty.
© 2023 The National Council for Civil Liberties

www.libertyhumanrights.org.uk

When will Sadiq Khan admit that stop and search works?

Even as London faces record knife killings, the Mayor continues to undermine a system that has a proven record of tackling crime.

By Shaun Bailey

Ask yourself this question today: do you feel safe in London? Then ask the person next to you, and then ask the person next to them, and keep going until someone says 'yes'. It may take some time.

Until every community can live, work, sleep, play and raise a family in our capital without fear, we cannot afford to stop being outraged about crime in the capital. Young boys being stabbed to death ought to be a rarity, yet in too many communities it is an expectation, with parents constantly worried about their children either joining a gang or being murdered by one.

The latest figures show that the black Londoners make up around 13 per cent of our city's population, but when it comes to the representation of victims of knife crime, that percentage shoots up to about 45 per cent, and 61 per cent of the perpetrators are black. Such figures are having an extraordinary real-world impact: let's never forget the tragic killings of 30 young people in 2021.

So what is to be done? We already know at least part of the answer. Out of the nearly 212,000 stop and searches carried out in 2021/22, some 26.4 per cent resulted in action. That accounts for around 56,000 crimes that would otherwise have remained undetected. Out of the 834,670 crimes recorded in London in the same year, some 7 per cent would not have come to light without stop and search. Such figures might seem marginal in the grand scheme of things, but they make an enormous difference.

Stop and search is both a deterrent to carrying weapons and a means to remove those weapons from our streets, but it requires strong political support to work properly – something it certainly hasn't received during Sadiq Khan's time as Mayor. The number of crimes solved in London (or sanction detection rate) has fallen from 19.3 per cent to only 8.7 per cent in 2021, despite there being more police on the streets than at any point in almost 20 years.

It is more than clear therefore that the issue is not a lack of resources but a lack of direction from Mr Khan. He needs to take more responsibility for ending the epidemic of murdered and incarcerated black Londoners, having shirked his responsibility as the overall Police and Crime Commissioner for the capital. Although this task isn't made easier by his damaged relationship with the Met Police. There has been rightful anger at his shoddy handling of Cressida Dick's resignation just months after being involved in negotiating her contract extension.

Too often on this critical issue, leaders have talked and listened only at election time, as a routine exercise to get voters – especially in the black community – to tick the box for the politician. This has not only made a mockery of the rule of law, but further still has allowed violent gangsters to continue to run rampage and take young lives.

We now need to push ahead with Intelligence-led stop and search. Police officers must be further trained and if necessary retrained to deal effectively with weapons and illegal drugs. And we can go further, too, in tackling the root causes of crime within our communities, through schemes that show that there is value in aspiration – and that generational poverty need not be guaranteed poverty.

Shaun Bailey is a London Assembly Member and the former Conservative candidate for Mayor of London.

17 May 2022

The above information is reprinted with kind permission from *The Telegraph*.
© Telegraph Media Group Limited 2022

www.telegraph.co.uk

Forgotten voices: Policing, stop and search and the perspectives of Black children

Report authors: Amber Evans, Strategy and Insight Manager | Patrick Olajide, Analyst | Isabella Ross, Junior Analyst | Jon Clements, Executive Director of Development

Our latest research has found that only 36 per cent of Black children and teenagers trust the police compared with 75 per cent of young White people. The trust figure for Black people aged ten to 18 was the lowest of any ethnic group and was even lower among Black Caribbean children.

Less than a quarter of Black children and teenagers questioned for the poll said they trusted police to stop and search them fairly and fewer than one in five trusted officers to treat people from different backgrounds fairly. The survey also suggests young Black people are less likely to call the police if they are in danger than those who are White or Black adults.

This research is the second of three reports, funded by the Hadley Trust, and considers children's experiences and views of policing and stop-and-search. The first study, published in November, focused on adults. It found that despite support for the principle of stop-and-search, there were deep misgivings among Black adults about the way the powers were used and how they were treated by police, in general.

In focus groups, conducted alongside the latest survey, Black and mixed ethnicity children said they wanted to trust the police but felt unable to do so because of negative interactions they or people close to them had experienced or viewed online.

One young teenager said: 'There's almost like an arrogance in the police. And it's almost like, we're going to, we don't have to talk to you properly, we're going to talk at you, not to you. Sometimes it's almost like a wind up as well.'

Another child told researchers: 'People who live in the nice houses, they think the police are there to protect them. People who live in the ghetto are mostly thinking that the police are out to get them. They know that they're gonna get stopped.'

Key findings of the survey of children and teenagers, aged ten to 18:

- 73% of respondents said they trust the police, compared with 62% in the adult survey
- 36% of young Black people trust the police; 75% for those who are White
- Only 28% of Black Caribbean children and teenagers said they trust the police
- Trust in the police was lower among older children and girls, with Black girls the lowest of all among those surveyed, at 33%
- 58% of all children and teenagers who had been stopped and searched said they trust the police, compared with 74% of those who had not been stopped
- Young people in the East Midlands and Greater London had the lowest levels of trust in the police

Crest Advisory Chief Executive Harvey Redgrave said:

'Our findings suggest that children and teenagers have conflicting views on the police and the trust they can place in them. The most alarming results from our survey are that levels of trust are much lower among young Black people, particularly those from Black Caribbean backgrounds.

'Contentious examples of racism and discrimination within policing, alongside the use of police powers, such as stop-and-search, were cited by children across the focus groups as reasons why their trust in the police had declined. These children now felt unsure as to whether they could truly trust the police,' he said.

Other key findings from the survey:

- 40% of Black children and teenagers, and 25% from Black Caribbean backgrounds, said they felt safe around the police compared with 75% of those who are White
- 66% of young Black people said they would call police if in danger compared with 87% of White children and teenagers
- 64% of White children and teenagers said knowing police are stopping and searching people in their area made them feel safer - but only 36% of young Black people said it did
- 25% of Black children and teenagers trust police to use stop-and-search fairly, compared with 51% of those who are White

One young teenager in a focus group said: 'I think that overall, stop and search is a good thing. Because at the moment there's a lot of knife crime, there's a lot of unnecessary death… but then at the same time, they get carried away with it, and then everyone they see is a potential gang member. And it's just not the case.'

Another focus group participant described what happened during a stop-and-search:

'I was coming out of the shop. And the policeman said, "come out of the shop" and then the police guy went all the way around and came back and stopped me and said when I came out of the shop, I put something in my pocket. Yeah. I came out of the shop. You took that as a reason to search. I felt so violated, I was thinking this ain't right. But if I do anything, they're gonna say I'm violent (…) Then what happened halfway through it, they were on the radio, and then they're like okay bye and just went.'

Redgrave said: 'Most children and teenagers said they would feel safer knowing police were stopping and searching people in their area, but this varied substantially by ethnicity. Most Black children said what they knew about stop-and-search had made them trust the police less.

'It is also clear that many children find the experience traumatic and further analysis is needed in this area to understand the long term effects of this.'

1 December 2022

The above information is reprinted with kind permission from Crest Advisory.
© 2023 Crest Advisory

www.crestadvisory.com

Boy gangster recruited when he was 12 makes desperate plea for help to get out

By Jordan King

A teenage boy appealed for help online and asked for advice on how to get out of a gang he has been involved with for four years.

A 16-year-old posted on Reddit that he does not know how to get out of a gang he was recruited into when he was only 12. He said his father died when he was young and his mother works seven days a week to support him and his younger brother.

He posted on the anonymous chat room that he had stabbed people, robbed people, sold drugs, been stabbed himself and spent time in a Young Offenders Institution.

He said: 'I don't want to live this life anymore but I don't know what to do.

'My best friend got stabbed to death last year and I have another friend in a wheelchair.

'Three of my friends are going to trial over a murder and two others are doing over five years.'

Ex-gang-member and consultant at charity Gangsline, Sheldon Thomas, said that with no father figure and a struggling family, boys like the anonymous poster are easy prey for gangs looking for new recruits.

Sheldon told Metro.co.uk that boys like the one who posted online have already been failed 'by everyone' and that drastic measures are needed to turn their lives around.

Having spoken to over 7,000 gang members as an activist, he said the only way for a child to get out of a gang is to move to another area – either with their families or by declaring themselves homeless – or through a mediation.

A mediation is when trained consultants negotiate someone's exit with a gang's elders to avoid repercussions.

But Sheldon says the Government and local authorities do not prioritise paying for such a process, making it more likely for children to stay trapped in a world of violence.

He told Metro.co.uk: 'Rather than pay me they would rather use teachers or the police service, who most young people don't like even if they are not in a gang.

'Most school teachers are middle-class white teachers. What on earth could they tell a young person to avoid when they don't even know what it's like to be in a gang?

'They don't know what it's like to live in an area where gangs control. They don't know what it's like to live in a house with no father figure.

'This kid should be able to phone me and I should have the funding to get one of my workers down there but I don't have the funding for that because the Government tells people lies.'

'From postcode to profit'

Research at London South Bank University suggests gang culture has changed from 'postcodes to profit', with the priority shifting from 'protecting territory from outsiders' to making money by selling drugs.

Sheldon said current gangs recruit children as part of their 'business model', using them to do 'the dirty work' such as selling drugs and carrying weapons, because they will serve less time if the police catch them.

He said: 'I was in gangs in the early 80s and in the early 80s you didn't groom children because you weren't allowed to.

'If you were found grooming children or sexually exploiting girls the crime families who controlled the gangs back then would have you killed.

'Grooming children is a new thing and over the last 15 years it's gotten really bad.'

The Government's anti-knife crime community fund, giving £30,000 to successful applicants looking to launch projects in their communities, is now in its third year.

But Sheldon says organisations like his do not have the money 'to pay somebody to fill in an application form for funding that looks like a dissertation'.

The consultant said that without funding for mediation the only way for the boy who shared his heartbreaking story to start a new life would be to move to another area.

Sheldon added: 'If he lives in North London he should move to South London because the gang is unlikely to look for him in South London. That's the only way he can cut ties.

'And when he moves he can't have the same phone number and he can't be on social media.'

Sheldon thinks the most important battle is preventing children from joining gangs in the first place, by getting organisations to children younger than 11 'so they know what to look out for when they get to secondary school'.

He added: 'We've been telling the mayor and the home office that this problem is going to get worse.

'I am a former gang member, I have engaged more gangs than every police force in this country and they told me I was exaggerating.'

The anonymous teenager confessed he was worried about his younger brother dabbling in gang culture. Sheldon encouraged both to contact organisations like Gangsline where ex-gang members can give them advice.

A report from the Office of National Statistics estimated that in 2018 there were 28,296 children between the ages of 10 and 16 who were part of a gang, with only 6,560 known to youth offending teams.

14 October 2020

The above information is reprinted with kind permission from *Metro*.
© 2023 Associated Newspapers Ltd

www.metro.co.uk

Key Facts

- In 2018 there were 28,296 children between the ages of 10 and 16 who were part of a gang, with only 6,560 known to youth offending teams

I was stabbed and surrounded by gangs at school – this is how to stop these attacks

We need school systems that provide opportunities for staff to build relationships, and have a greater understanding of the local context they work in.

By Mohamed Abdallah

The two young men stopped me on my way home. I was near my home in southeast London, walking back after a long day of work at about 7pm in the evening.

Give me your phone, he says.

Ridiculously, I reply 'no'. I was too old for this kind of thing. I knew people like this. I had once known people like this too well.

I said again, I'm not going to give you my phone.

That's when I thought he was punching me very hard in the leg. But it wasn't a punch. He had stabbed me with a knife.

There was a tussle between us, and this guy and his friend ran off. It wasn't until I got home I began to process what had happened, and I called an ambulance.

Last week, the government announced a 'crackdown against organised criminal gangs'. The home secretary, Suella Braverman, has launched a consultation on this.

The Home Office is proposing that police 'ruthlessly pursue' criminal gang members, 'maintain grip' on the area, and then 'build' the community to be more prosperous.

I'm not here to say if that's the right approach or not. But I hope my experience gives an insight into how you make a real difference to young people who are most likely to be affected by gangs.

I am a school leader, working with students who experienced real vulnerability and disadvantage. I'm also one of the few school leaders with personal experience of gangs.

A close relative of mine was in a gang in south London. When I was a child, people would come up to me and my brothers and ask us to pass on messages to this relative. Sometimes they were threatening messages.

One time, in retaliation, a group of boys broke into our home and attacked our family with a hammer, and threw another relative down the stairs. Fortunately, there was no long-lasting physical damage, but seeing that as a child had a long-lasting emotional impact.

In school, me and my brothers never showed anything that was going on outside the gates. We were quiet children, who behaved pretty well. None of the teachers knew what was going on.

That's because there was a culture of 'what happens at home stay at home'; and that mentality was very strong.

As a result, and because we didn't present with challenging behaviours, the teachers thought we were good kids with good lives. They assumed we just hung out with some 'bad kids' – but these other students weren't bad children. They were our friends, caught up in very tricky circumstances.

Of course, all the stress did impact me. I didn't do very well in my GCSEs, which was a surprise, because I had been good in school when I was younger. But I just wasn't engaged. My mind was often elsewhere, because I was on the periphery of these gangs.

You will have heard of county lines, which describes drugs being transported from one area to another (often from the city to countryside), usually through children.

That is not a new phenomenon. Anyone my age who grew up like I did will tell you that's not new at all.

Buying you trainers, nice food, a new coat, offering protection – this was all happening when I was a teenager. It was to groom children into transporting drugs and entering gang life.

I have friends who were murdered. I have friends with significant mental health issues. I have close friends who have been in and out of prison.

What was different for me?

I was lucky enough that I had a family who were financially okay. I had many more opportunities presented to me, and that was a stronger pull than the gang (which is like a replacement family for some people). My friends without that kind of financial stability and access to opportunities fell into gangs.

So of course, we can do 'crackdowns' on criminal gang leaders. But as long as there are children out there without real opportunities to realise their purpose, there will be criminal gang leaders waiting to offer alternatives.

There is a way to break the cycle, though, and that is to really understand these children when they go through the one place we are able to meet them on their level – school.

But too many of us in school talk about these children as 'vulnerable'. We describe their communities as being 'disadvantaged', 'broken' or 'destitute'.

Although well intentioned, this deficit approach causes unintended harm to these children and their communities.

Firstly, it defines children and their communities by what they don't have rather than what they have in abundance. An abundance of connections, relationships, knowledge, qualities and skills that make them incredibly resilient in the face of challenge.

Secondly, children and their communities internalise the idea that they are 'vulnerable', 'disadvantaged' or 'broken', and that they can only be fixed by others who are from the outside of their community.

Another problem is that we have schools staffed by adults who are unfamiliar with the local community.

In fact, there is often a clear distinction between those staff from working class backgrounds, and those who aren't. The people who know the local community are often canteen staff, learning support assistants and reception staff – those without any decision-making power in the school.

The people in positions of leadership – headteachers, deputy headteachers – do not often have a lived experience within the local communities of their schools.

This means that schools and communities can find it hard to connect with one another.

When that happens students may feel the school doesn't really understand them or their context, and they reject it, or (like me) they withdraw from it.

To overcome this, we first need to acknowledge the challenge and then create real opportunities to build meaningful relationships.

As the head of the Inclusive Leadership Course at The Difference, I am now committed to supporting school leaders to create schools which improve outcomes and opportunities for all students and staff.

This also needs support at a policy level. We need government incentives that make wellbeing and inclusion of students equally as important as academic outputs.

And we need school systems that provide opportunities for staff to build relationships, and have a greater understanding of the local context they work in. To move from a deficit to an asset-based approach involves meaningful curiosity about every student, who they are, and what matters to them.

At The Difference we are committed to supporting schools to help them discover the wealth of knowledge and skills they have in their communities, and understand how this could be used to improve their inclusion and safeguarding offer.

Thinking back to when I got stabbed that day, I wasn't mad at the guy who had done it. I was in a position where I had a good idea of why people behaved in that way.

Schools need to reflect their communities, not reject them. We need to use the language of assets, not the language of deficit. And we need incentives in the system to change.

Only then can you start to break the cycle of gang grooming.

Mohamed Abdallah is the head of the inclusive leadership course at The Difference.

19 February 2023

Activity

Do you think that your school reflects the community that you live in?

How can teachers and senior leadership at your school get to know about the local community?

What do you want them to know about life outside of school?

Write down some things that your school can improve on, and areas that they do well on.

The above information is reprinted with kind permission from *The Independent*.
© independent.co.uk 2023

www.independent.co.uk

Sport can help to reduce youth offending but the evidence around what works is problematic

Football and other sports are often used as a sport-based intervention – a tool for promoting social inclusion, personal development and youth crime prevention.

Its advocates claim that taking part in sport and physical activity can engage young people in developmental opportunities which empower them and impact positively on outcomes including mental and physical health, life skills, educational achievement and employability.

Furthermore, SBIs are increasingly being used in attempts to reduce youth offending particularly within the context of youth violence.

However, new research by academics from Loughborough University has shown that measuring the success of sport-based interventions (SBIs) is complex and problematic.

The team has found that the metrics used to indicate success, by funders, organisers and those in the justice sector – such as sessions attended, qualifications gained and increase in confidence – do not necessarily align with the aspirations of young people.

Elements such as the quality of sessions, enjoyment and relationship building are much more important to youngsters.

Dr Carolynne Mason, of Loughborough's School of Sport, Exercise and Health Sciences, said that there is tension between what funders expect delivery organisations to measure, and the value of SBIs when seen from the perspectives of the young people who take part.

She said: 'We have argued that enhancing the evidence around the impact of SBIs, requires a shift in mindset away from adult-centric evidential concerns which fail to acknowledge children's viewpoints.

'We have further argued that funders and policymakers may need to relinquish their desire for the production of particular types of evidence simply because such desires fail to recognize the complex everyday life experiences of young people who offend or acknowledge the unique journeys upon which they embark.'

Dr Mason also highlighted young people's reservations about giving personal details to figures of authority – another factor that likely contributes to poor data gathering, that needs to be addressed.

She said: 'Children and young people, who are less powerful than adults, are often sceptical about revealing information that might be used against them and in the context of preventing and reducing youth offending their suspicions are heightened about the motivations of researchers and other adults particularly where their families are known to statutory services.

'Mistrust, low literacy levels and not wanting to disclose personal information all make using surveys with this target group challenging. Surveys designed to record impact across a narrow range of predefined dimensions to justify the initial financial investment in the intervention, often fail to demonstrate the impact that matters most to the children and young people in the programmes and therefore their voices are excluded from the evidence base.'

In response to these challenges, a qualitative visual data collection tool which is based around a teenage cartoon-style pro-social sporting journey poster has been developed by the research team at Loughborough.

The innovative poster is based on academic insight from the criminal and youth justice sector as well as insight from a number of research projects undertaken by the research team and builds on the Theory of Change for *'Using Sport to Enhance Positive Outcomes for Young People in the Context of Serious Youth Violence' A Theory of Change | StreetGames* (Mason, Walpole and Case, 2020).

This Theory of Change has already started to have a significant impact in the field and has been adopted nationally by StreetGames and more recently, by the Ministry of Justice as the framework for its recent £5 million Youth Justice Sports Fund funding.

The poster was initially developed by the research team – with the support of Dr Lesley Sharpe, from the University of Lincoln – in partnership with StreetGames as an engagement tool for referral agencies working with young people at risk of involvement in Serious Youth Violence (SYV).

Dr Mason said: 'The poster is about engaging the young person in normative, pro-social opportunities with an emphasis on their strengths, making positive decisions and choices, benefits, achievements and future aspirations.

'These have the potential to contribute to the development of a pro-social identity, viewed as important in terms of preventing and reducing offending.

'Using a co-creation approach, the poster's value is currently being piloted by Dr Caron Walpole with young people living in the East Midlands who will have the opportunity to refine the evaluation tool based on their experiences.'

19 May 2023

The above information is reprinted with kind permission from Loughborough University.
© 2023 Loughborough University

www.lboro.ac.uk

Coalition calls for alternative solutions to serious youth violence

New report launched by campaigners and grassroots groups say government neglect is damaging communities and investment in young people is needed.

- Groups call for a new approach to serious youth violence, including better funded youth services and a rolling back of police powers to build trust with communities
- Meanwhile 7 in 10 members of the public (69%) say the government needs to look for solutions that tackle the root causes of violence, and three quarters (74%) want to see more funding for youth services

A groundbreaking report launched today by a coalition of grassroots groups and campaigning organisations has called for a new approach to tackling serious youth violence, with the powers of the police rolled back and more funding and support given for young people to thrive. The groups argue that the government are harming communities by failing to invest in young people, and say that the policing of young people, particularly young people of colour, is damaging their futures.

Authored by nine organisations working across human rights, youth safety, racial justice, mental health and policing, *Holding Our Own: A guide to non-policing solutions to serious youth violence* advocates for major investment in trauma-informed and racially literate support for young people to prevent harm, build trusting relationships and support them with issues they face. The Report also calls attention to the ways in which the rhetoric around – and subsequent government action towards – serious youth violence continues to be underpinned by racism and ignorance around its root causes.

Education is central to the proposed new approach, with the report calling for an end to school exclusions, the removal of police from schools, and better training for teachers to understand the needs of pupils experiencing racism and discrimination. It also calls for an end to drugs policing, an end to racist joint enterprise prosecutions, and for greater justice and accountability following deaths in police custody.

Meanwhile, new polling figures show a high level of support for more funding to support young people. Three quarters (74%) want to see the government spending more on funding for youth services, and the same number say they are concerned by the impact of cuts to these kinds of services – with funding cut by 70% over the past decade.

The polling figures, released today, also reveal high levels of concern about policing in the UK, with four in five members of the public (81%) concerned about police officers abusing their power.

Police abuse of power, and particularly their treatment of young people of colour, has come under intense scrutiny

in recent months following the strip search of a Black schoolgirl known as Child Q while on her period. A recent report by the Children's Commissioner found widespread abuse of the power to strip search children, with thousands of children strip searched since 2018. In over half of cases, no appropriate adult was present. The report also found that Black children were eleven times more likely to be strip searched than their white peers.

Martha Spurrier, Director of Liberty, said:

'Whatever our postcode or the colour of our skin, we all deserve to grow up in communities where we are cared for, and given the tools we need to flourish in life.

'But instead of investing in young people or providing support to deal with the causes of social problems, the government has given the police more powers to try and tackle the symptoms of these issues. This has led to more and more people being treated unfairly by the police, rather than being given the help they need.

'Our communities need investment, so that together we can create spaces and services that we know will give our young people the best chance in life. And we need to roll back the powers of the police so no-one faces harsh and traumatising treatment at the hands of police.

'*Holding Our Own*, launched today, provides a vital blueprint for how we can undo the harm currently being done to our communities, and instead build a society where all children are given the chance to thrive.'

A spokesperson for the National Survivor User Network (NSUN) said:

'We're so energised by this joint call for community-led solutions to what gets called serious youth violence.

'Often, we see calls for increased and expanded mental health services as something that could help tackle the root causes of violence. Our contribution focuses on the ways in which traditional mental health services can be places where people face violence through coercion and restrictive practice.

'We call for resourced community care so that communities can respond to distress in ways that prioritise care, choice, and freedom.'

Andre Gomes, Communications Lead at Release, the UK's national centre of expertise on drugs and drug law, said:

'It's widely understood that the drug war has failed to control drug related harms, having instead become a mechanism of state and racialised control over minority communities in the UK.

'The criminalisation of drugs and their policing create an excuse for police to harass, strip, and traumatise young people of colour.

'The decriminalisation of drugs, which has already been implemented in over 30 countries, would be the first step towards removing police presence from people's lives, and set the path to fund other non-carceral activities.'

Jessica Pandian, on behalf of the charity INQUEST, said:

'Serious youth violence is directly linked to the state's long-standing marginalisation of working-class young people and the decimation of youth services of which deaths in custody are at the sharpest end. Over our 40 year history, we have worked with countless bereaved families of young people who have died police-related deaths.

'Young Black people are disproportionately likely to die police-related deaths. Furthermore, their deaths have revealed racial stereotyping, equating young people with criminality and dangerousness, and use of racist narratives around gangs and drugs. This strongly reflects the systemic anti-Black racism embedded in policing policy and practice. In addition, the deaths of women have exposed the institutional sexism and misogyny in policing.

'In the short term, we need to make the post-death processes more truthful, just and accountable. In the long term, it is imperative that we move away from policing as a response to social problems and invest in communities.'

25 April 2023

> **Discuss...**
>
> In small groups, discuss ways to tackle youth violence. Brainstorm things that can help with the causes of youth violence.

The above information is reprinted with kind permission from Liberty.
© 2023 Liberty

www.libertyhumanrights.org.uk

What's the solution to youth crime?

Two in five say youth crime is a major issue in the UK, but the public favours increased funding for rehabilitation over jail time.

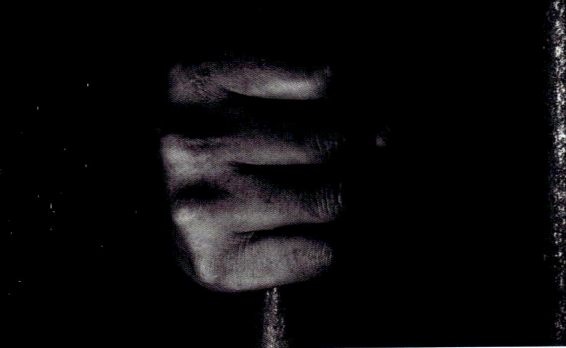

With knife crime at an all-time high, London mayoral candidate Rory Stewart has promised to triple police numbers in the capital if elected, and Boris Johnson is launching a new task force to crack down on county lines gangs - but do Britons think more Bobbies on the beat is the best solution?

Is youth crime a national, local problem, or a London problem?

From a local perspective, the problem is concentrated in the capital – with Londoners twice as likely to say their area has a major issue with youth crime compared to the national average.

Six in ten (61%) Londoners say the capital has at least somewhat of a problem with young people and crime – with 23% saying it's a major issue.

Outside the capital, 48% of Britons in the north of England say their local area has somewhat of a problem, but only 9% say it's a major one, and further afield only 36% of Scots say their local area has somewhat of an issue. Just 3% say Scotland has a major issue with young people involved in crime.

However, looking at the national picture, Britons are much more likely to see youth crime as a major issue for the UK as a whole. Overall 86% of Brits think the UK has at least somewhat of a problem with youth crime, split down the middle with 43% ranking the issue as major.

Do Britons think youth crime is a national or local problem?

To what extent, if at all, do you think youth crime is an issue for...?
(%, those who said 'Don't know' not shown)

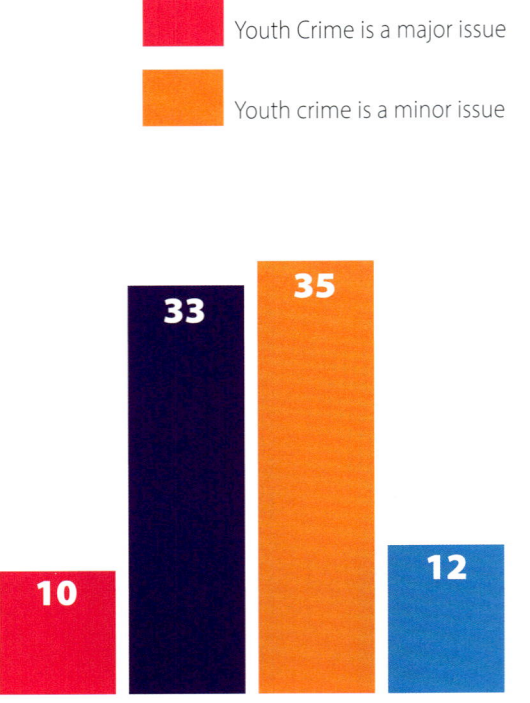

Source: YouGov 19-20 January 2020

issues: Youth Violence   38   Chapter 3: Tackling Youth Crime

How do voters think youth crime should be tackled?

Thinking about youth crime, in your opinion which of the following options are the best ways to discourage children becoming involved in crime? (select up to three) (%)

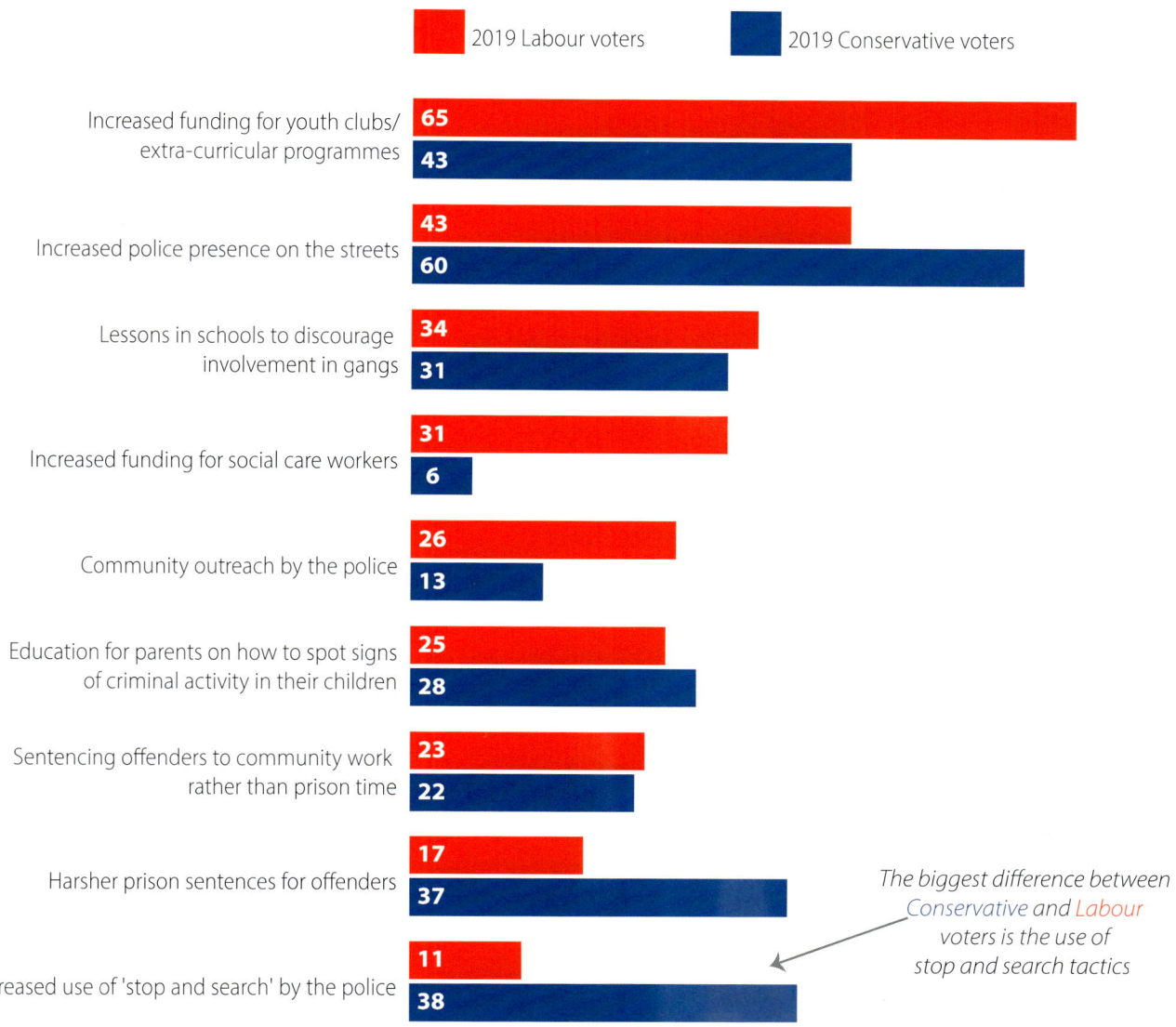

The biggest difference between Conservative and Labour voters is the use of stop and search tactics

Source: YouGov 19-20 January 2020

Conservative voters are the most likely to see the country has having an issue with youth crime, with 51% saying it is a major issue compared to 38% of Labour voters and 31% of Liberal Democrats.

How do Britons think we should tackle youth crime?

Despite promises of more police on the streets by politicians - voters are split over the best way to tackle the issue.

Those who backed the Labour Party at the 2019 general election are more likely to in favour of preventative schemes and improving social care, with the most popular solution among labour voters being increasing funding for youth clubs and extracurricular programmes – however, 43% still say that an increased police presence on the streets would be one of the most effective ways to discourage crime among youth.

This is compared to Conservative voters, who listed increased police officer numbers as their most effective solution at 60%. Conservative voters are also twice as likely to support longer custodial sentences for youth offenders (37%) compared to Labour voters (17%), and three times as likely to support increased use of the controversial 'stop and search' tactics (38%) than Labour voters (11%).

Britons who say the issue of youth crime is a major issue for the UK are the most likely to be in favour of increasing police numbers - 60% compared to 49% of Britons overall - and upping the length of prison sentences for offenders – 42% compared to 29% of Britons overall.

12 February 2020

Activity

Create a questionnaire to find out your friend's and family's opinions on how to tackle youth crime. Do the results differ from the findings by the YouGov survey?

The above information is reprinted with kind permission from YouGov.
© 2023 YouGov PLC

www.yougov.co.uk

Agony of mum whose teen son lost his life to knife crime

She still feels he could 'walk through the door any minute'.

By Helen Kreft, Senior reporter

The mother of a Derbyshire teen who was stabbed to death says she is still grieving the loss of her son and feels he could return home at any point. 17-year-old Benjamin Orton was stabbed to death by Eric Rudaks, then 16, in a Swadlincote alleyway at the Pipeworks.

Benjamin was treated by paramedics at the scene, but sadly died of his injuries on June 12 last year. He had been walking through the centre when a confrontation took place between themselves and Rudaks, reports Staffordshire Live.

Both Benjamin and Rudaks were carrying knives at the time of the incident. Rudaks went on to be convicted of manslaughter and sentenced to 12 years detention after a trial at Derby Crown Court.

Now, as part of the ongoing Operation Sceptre launched by police nationwide to tackle knife crime, Benjamin's mother, Amanda Orton-Taylor, has joined forces with Swadlincote police safer neighbourhood team. The team took part in knife amnesties, park sweeps, test purchase operations, school visits and targeting those that, intelligence suggested, were carrying knives.

Officers also joined Benjamin's mother at a memorial site set up in his memory at The Pipeworks shopping centre. She said: 'It still feels like Benji will walk through the door at any minute. If I can get one message out to anyone carrying a knife or thinking of carrying a knife; don't.

'I don't want anyone else going through what me, my family and friends have been through and have to live with.'

Rudaks was only 16 when he stabbed 17-year-old Benjamin 13 times. A trial last year heard that in the process he pierced Benjamin's lung and heart in the incident next to the Odeon cinema in the town, leaving him fatally injured.

Rudaks was jailed for 12 years on Friday, January 14, with the court hearing emotional words from Benjamin's mum, Staffordshire Live reports.

In a heartfelt statement, Ms Orton-Taylor told Derby Crown Court that Rudaks, has 'stolen' her son's life.

In a victim impact statement read to the court, she said: 'His death still doesn't seem real to me and I still expect him to come home every day. It has had a huge impact on our younger son. He misses Ben helping with his computer and bickering. He has not gone to school since he died and fears jitties and alleyways.'

Rudaks had pleaded not guilty to charges of murder, manslaughter and attempted murder. He also denied causing grievous bodily harm with intent to Benjamin's friend, Joe McMullen.

But after a four-week trial in December, 2021, a jury convicted him of manslaughter. He was cleared of the other charges. He appeared to be sentenced.

Mr McMullen was stabbed five times by Rudaks and survived, but was left with life-changing injuries when one of the stab wounds pierced his spinal cord, the court had been told.

Judge Thomas Linden QC told Rudaks today: 'This comes as close to murder as it is possible to come without a conviction for murder.'

The court had been told Rudaks and Benjamin had met at The Pingle Academy, in Swadlincote, where they were both pupils. Initially they were friends, but had a falling out when Benjamin wanted Rudaks to beat up a drug dealer and Rudaks refused, the court heard.

On the day Benjamin died, he and Mr McMullen had followed Rudaks and others down the alley when a confrontation happened, which led to Rudaks pulling a knife - as did Benjamin, the jury was told.

In her statement, Mrs Taylor-Orton said: 'When I hear parents talking about their bickering child, I say "don't knock it", because when it's gone, you'll miss it.

'We lost my brother two years ago. My mother believes you should never go before your children - even more so when losing a grandchild.'

Write

'If I can get one message out to anyone carrying a knife or thinking of carrying a knife; don't.

I don't want anyone else going through what me, my family and friends have been through and have to live with.'

Using the above quote, write an essay on why people shouldn't carry knives.

In her statement, she also criticised the court's verdict, saying she felt it 'got stuck in the jury's head' that her son was a gang member when he was not.

She said: 'I couldn't understand the jury's verdict of manslaughter. I don't understand how someone could stab someone multiple times and not intend to kill them.

'Before he died, I was always ready to go out, even when I wasn't [going out], but now I don't want to get out of bed. I don't see the point. I don't feel I have any purpose.

'I was robbed of Ben's future. Erik Rudaks has stolen his life and his family's lives. I will never be right again. I am absolutely disgusted that there is no justice for Joe McMullen.'

She said the verdict seemed to suggest it was ok to stab someone.

Judge Linden told the court that there was a 'growing number of victims of reckless behaviour by youths carrying knives'.

He also said no amount of sentencing could bring Benjamin back to his family.

He told Rudaks: 'Benjamin and Joe McMullen had spotted you [in the alleyway] and followed you with no good reason for doing so. Ben was carrying a knife and you were also carrying a knife.

'The CCTV footage shows you and Benjamin both pull knives but you rapidly became the aggressor and they began backing away.

'The jury was sure this was not a case of self defence but they were not sure you intended to cause serious harm.

'You barrister said your actions carried a high risk of serious harm or death and I agree.

'I am sure when the violence started you were the aggressor. You decided to fight rather than walk away.'

24 May 2022

The above information is reprinted with kind permission from DerbyshireLive.
© 2023 Local World

www.derbytelegraph.co.uk

Useful Websites

Useful Websites

www.benkinsella.org.uk

www.btp.police.uk

www.catch-22.org.uk

www.childrenssociety.org.uk

www.crestadvisory.com

www.derbytelegraph.co.uk

www.independent.co.uk

www.lboro.ac.uk

www.libertyhumanrights.org.uk

www.lifeorknife.west-midlands.police.uk

www.metro.co.uk

www.nacro.org.uk

www.parliament.uk

www.shoutoutuk.org

www.telegraph.co.uk

www.thecommissiononyounglives.co.uk

www.theconversation.com

www.victimsupport.org.uk

www.wearencs.com

www.yougov.co.uk

Where can I find help?

Below are some telephone numbers, email addresses and websites of agencies or charities that can offer support or advice if you, or someone you know, needs it.

Childline
www.childline.org.uk
0800 1111

Crimestoppers
www.crimestoppers-uk.org
0800 555 111

Is This OK?
www.isthisok.org.uk/get-support/

The Ben Kinsella Trust
www.benkinsella.org.uk

Victim Support
www.victimsupport.org.uk
08 08 16 89 111

If you or someone you know is in immediate danger, you should contact emergency services by phoning 999

Glossary

Age of criminal responsibility
The minimum age of criminal responsibility in England and Wales was set at ten in the 1963 Children and Young Person's Act. In the 1998 Crime and Disorder Act, Labour abolished the principle of doli incapax, whereby the prosecution had to prove that a child under 14 appearing in the criminal court knew and fully understood what he or she was doing was seriously wrong.

Baiting
A method of provocation. To intentionally make someone angry by doing or saying things to annoy them.

Bullying
A form of aggressive behaviour used to intimidate someone. It can be inflicted both physically and mentally (psychologically).

County lines
'County lines' is a term used to describe criminal gangs from big cities who expand their operations to smaller towns. They groom and exploit children and vulnerable people to traffick and sell drugs for them.

Crime
Crime may be defined as an act or omission prohibited or punished by law. A 'criminal offence' includes any infringement of the criminal law, from homicide to riding a bicycle without lights. What is classified as a crime is supposed to reflect the values of society and to reinforce those values. If an act is regarded as harmful to society or its citizens, it is often, but not always, classified as a criminal offence.

Crime Survey for England & Wales (CSEW)
The Crime Survey for England and Wales (CSEW) is an organised study of national crime trends. It measures the levels and types of crime in England and Wales by asking people about whether they or members of their households have experienced any crimes in the past year.

Cuckooing
The process through which county lines operators take over a local property to use as a base for their criminal activity. The operators usually target and exploit vulnerable people such as those dependent on drugs, with mental health issues, or the elderly. Through the use of violence, intimidation, or coercion (i.e. by offering money or drugs in exchange for use of their property), the operators then take over the property, sometimes rendering the victim homeless in the process.

Dealing
Supplying drugs to another person, usually in return for money. However, giving drugs away free to friends is also classed as dealing, and is subject to the same penalties as selling drugs. Dealing illegal drugs carries greater penalties than possession for personal use.

Deterrent
Any threat or punishment which is seen to deter someone from a certain action: the threat of prison, for example, is expected to function as a deterrent to criminal behaviour.

Drill and Grime
A genre of music often linked to gang violence due to its lyrical content.

Exploitation
Taking advantage of or using someone for selfish reasons.

Gangs
Gangs are groups of people, often young people who hang around together. They often have a bad reputation as they can sometimes be involved in anti-social or criminal behaviour. Territorial by nature, they are often in violent conflict with gangs from neighbouring areas.

Knife crime
'Knife' crime is crime involving a knife or an object with a blade or a sharp instrument. It's a crime to threaten someone with a knife or carry a knife as a weapon in a robbery or burglary. Police can search you if they think you're carrying a knife.

Racial discrimination
Racial discrimination occurs when a person is treated less favourably because of their colour, race, nationality or ethnic or national origins.

Risky behaviour
Behaviour that has the potential to get out of control or become dangerous.

Sentence
The punishment given by a judge to a convicted offender at the end of a criminal trial. This generally takes the form of a fine, a community punishment, a discharge or a period of imprisonment.

Social action
Social action is about people coming together to help improve their lives and solve the problems that are important in their communities.

Stop and search
There are different types of stop and search. Under section 1 of the Police and Criminal Evidence Act, stop and search requires officers to show they have 'reasonable grounds' to believe you're carrying a prohibited item before subjecting you to an invasive public search. But under section 60 of the Criminal Justice and Public Order Act, officers can, for a certain time period, carry out searches without ANY 'reasonable grounds'.

Street gangs
Criminal groups concerned with perpetuating a threat of violence or harm across a geographical area related to their main activities. Gangs tend to be less organised or co-ordinated than organised crime groups, but their criminal activity often overlaps.

Index

A
adverse childhood experiences 8–9
attitudes to youth crime 38–39
austerity 9

B
BAME people 2, 13, 29, 30, 37
Ben Kinsella Trust 6–7

C
coercive control 25
County lines 12, 16–17, 18, 20–24
criminal records 1, 7, 11

D
deaths 6–7, 40–41
drug trafficking *see* County lines
drugs, decriminalisation of 37

E
education 1, 7, 12, 36, 39
Equality Act 2010 28
exploitation of young people 17, 18, 19, 20, 21

F
families, impact on 6–7, 11, 40–41
fathers, absent 2, 31

G
gangs *see also* serious youth violence (SYV), tackling
    County lines 12, 17, 18, 20–24
    definition 14
    girls and young women 25
    joining 14–15, 16–17, 19, 33–34
    and knife crime 11, 12
    leaving 22–24, 31–32
    schools and 33–34
    victims of 15
girls and young women 25

I
injuries 6–7, 11
interventions to tackle youth offending 23–24, 33–37

J
Jay (County lines) 22–24

K
Kinsella, Ben 2, 3, 6–7
knife crime *see also* serious youth violence (SYV), tackling
    factors leading to 2, 8–9, 10, 12
    gangs and 11, 12
    law 1, 4–5, 7, 11, 12, 26–28
    and the media 13
    statistics 2, 3, 4–5, 29
    tackling 1, 7, 9, 12, 40
    victims 2, 6–7, 8, 12, 40–41

L
laws and knife crime 1, 4–5, 7, 11, 12, 26–28
London 13, 29, 38

M
Marie (mentor) 23–24
media 13, 21, 25
mental health 2, 11, 15
mentoring 23–24
Merseyside 16–17

N
NACRO 13
normalisation of carrying knives 3, 7

O
Orton, Benjamin 40–41

P
peer pressure 1, 10, 12, 14–15
police 12–13, 26–28, 30, 36–37
policing, increased 39
political affiliation and attitudes to youth crime 39

R
rappers 13
recruitment to County lines 20, 21, 22–23
rights, stop and search 27–28

S
sale of knives 3, 12
schools 8, 9, 33–34
Section 60 searches 27–28
self-defence 1
sentencing 39, 40–41
Serious Organised Crime Early Intervention Service 23–24
Serious Violence Reduction Orders (SVRO) 27
serious youth violence (SYV), tackling 35, 36–37
sexual assault 5
sexual exploitation 19, 25
social causes of youth violence 2, 8–9, 12, 16, 17, 33–34
social media 21, 25
social services 19, 39
sport-based initiatives (SBIs) 35
stop and search 11, 13, 26–27, 29, 30, 39
strip searches 36–37
support for victims 15

T
trends, knife crime 4–5

V
victims 2, 6–7, 8, 12, 15, 40–41
vulnerable young people 19, 20, 21, 22–23, 34

Y
youth services 9, 36–37, 39 *see also* sport-based initiatives (SBIs)